THE PSYCHOLOGY OF RACISM:
UNDERSTANDING ANTI-RACIST PROTEST

By Dr. Jerry Mungadze PhD

Introduction

Like many people in the United States, I watched in horror as a black man was pinned down to the ground, with his neck under the knee of a white police officer. The helpless man could be heard pleading with the officer, telling him that he couldn't breathe. I observed the other police officers involved in the incident – some actively participated by holding George Floyd down, while another stood by, watching it all. A group of civilian bystanders called on the officer to get off the man's neck, to no avail. The man's body went limp, and shortly after that, he died from the injury to his neck. Later on, autopsies confirmed that the death was due to police brutality.

I remember thinking to myself that this wasn't the first or only time that I had seen such incidents. Other black men have died, been beaten or wrongly arrested, also leading to protests against police brutality. These protests seem to have failed to prevent such abuses, as we continue to witness these horrific cases. I am beginning to worry that something different must take place to enact real change.

Watching the protests which are ongoing at this present time, I came to see that these protests are different from those of the past. Although the name of George Floyd is still a rallying cry, it appears that the focus is no longer on him, as protests have been ignited around the world. It is clear to me that this is about a much bigger issue, one that has been around for centuries – the role that race has played in human societies from the beginning of time.

If one listens to what is being said by reasonable voices, the protests are driven by racial tensions brought about by racial discrimination of various types. People are tired of racial discrimination wherever it is happening and everyone is paying the price. Riots, violence, loss of life and destruction of property and the economy are spreading across the globe, all because people cannot get along.

I am primarily interested in finding a solution to this problem that can work and bring us closer to each other, as opposed to dividing us even more. We can protest all we want, but that alone will not end racism. Riots and looting diminish the power of peaceful protesters and perpetuate the very hostility that we are trying to rid ourselves of. There is talk of defunding or abolishing the police, but that will not end racism. Changing laws that dictate how police function is a step in the right direction, but it will not end racism.

Racism goes deeper than police brutality and permeates all areas of human life. There is racism in education, police departments, workplaces, sports and even in our churches. If we want to end racism, we must look more deeply at world views and the religious and cultural biases that people have towards one another. Racism has its own life, philosophy and culture. We must begin by looking at this if we are to make any progress. The problem will not disappear overnight, and its solution will be a process that takes time – to assume otherwise would be unrealistic.

I have seen the emotion demonstrated both by the protesters and those who oppose them, and I realize that the solutions may not be found in these emotional responses. The emotion certainly has spoken to the depth of the hurt and frustration concerning racial injustice and police brutality. However, solutions must come from rational, calculated and meaningful dialogue between everyone involved. Leaders of law enforcement organizations, affected populations and white communities must collaborate in resolving these issues. A truly meaningful dialogue must look at racism objectively to get to the root of the issues.

Racism hurts everyone, even racists themselves, who carry an internal burden of bitterness and hate. Racism is like a cancer that needs treatment. As a mental health professional I am familiar with dealing with problems at their root. As I have already pointed out, racism is not limited to police brutality, but it is one of its causes. As a black person, I have also experienced my share of personal racial injustices and undeserved police profiling. I also grew up in Rhodesia (now Zimbabwe) under the racial system of Apartheid.

Due to my own journey with racial discrimination and experiences working with people with all sorts of trauma and problems, I believe that I have some insights as to how we could resolve this issue. The bottom line for me is that we need to start with a meaningful dialogue that looks at the nature and culture of racism. We have to look where we haven't looked before and try approaches that we haven't tried before. I understand there is a lot of pain from the past that includes pain from the legacy of slavery, racial discrimination and a great deal of ill treatment of one race by another. If we are going to end this vicious cycle, we must learn how to heal our wounds from the past rather than allow them to dictate our present and future.

The title of this book underscores the importance of understanding the mindset of racism in order to deal with it effectively. I want to address the matter at the heart of these protests that goes beyond what happened to George Floyd. It is clear that the same issues of racial injustice are occurring around the world. As you will see from my own experiences, this is a large issue and it is not confined to the United States of America.

I was born and raised in southern Africa during the great discriminatory system of government called Apartheid. This system segregated people according to race, with white people given all the power. They built houses, schools, cities and businesses centered around themselves. All black people were given places in what were called "reservations." Typically, these reservations had very poor soil and the portions of land given to them were very small, while white farmers were given huge pieces of the best land. In the cities, white people lived in nicer parts of town, while black people were pushed into terribly crowded areas that were called "townships." Black people provided labor for white people.

Black people composed the majority but had no say in the way that the country was run (or in any other matters). Other minorities, who were not black, were treated a little better than black people. However, under Apartheid, everyone lived with people of their own race and black people were not allowed to live where white people lived.

The treatment of black people was based on the assumption, mindset or psychology that black people were so inferior to white people that their lives did not matter much. The value of black people boiled down to manual labor. Some of the white churches even believed that black people didn't have souls and that there was no use to try to save them because they couldn't go to heaven. I grew up knowing that as black people, we were likened to baboons and monkeys. White people, not just the police, could harm black people with no legal consequences. Black lives didn't matter back then according to Apartheid. I have so many stories about discrimination and white brutality that if I were to tell the stories, they would fill the pages of another book.

Apartheid was born out of racism: the belief that white people were superior to and smarter than black people, who were considered to be stupid and ignorant. Black people were not believed to be able to govern themselves, only white people were considered competent to run a government. Everything was segregated because white people felt that black people would contaminate them and their community if they were allowed to intermingle. Schools, hospitals cemeteries, public transportation and every area of life was segregated. Even within a single city, the feeling was one of many different countries. I had many different experiences that continued to accentuate my awareness of Apartheid.

I remember that on one rainy day, my father and I were walking to our house on the farm of the white man that my father worked for.

The farmer drove his pickup truck past us on his way to his house. As he passed us (with no offer of a ride), my father observed that his gardener was riding in the bed of the truck, while the farmer's dog was riding in the cab. My wise father pointed this out to me and told me how wrong that was because a human being (though black) has more value than the dog. My father said that by the action of favoring the dog over the gardener, his boss saw the dog as more important than his gardener.

That same year one of my brothers was teaching at a Catholic school far away from our village. My father and I took the bus to my brother's school, but the bus left us almost 50 miles away from our destination. We had to walk in hope that someone with a car would offer us a ride the rest of the way. We had walked about 15 miles, my little legs were tired and hurting, and I was asking my father to try and stop all the cars passing us. However, all of the drivers were white people and we doubted that any of them would stop for us. Surprisingly, one stopped and we ran to the car. The driver was an older white man with clerical collar around the neck of his shirt which told me that he was a Catholic priest. He asked us to get into the car and offered the passenger seat to my father, which my father declined. My father asked me to sit in the front because he wanted me to talk to the white man since I could speak English. This white man took us all the way to my brother's school, which was significantly out of his way. I learned that day that some white people saw us black people as important enough to stop and give a ride.

The Apartheid system was dismantled in Zimbabwe in 1980, but by this time I had already left the country to come to the United States to study. I was fully expecting to be treated differently in the United States. The reason for such an expectation was that white American missionaries had treated me better than did the whites in my own country. However, it wasn't long before I realized that racism was also present in America, though not as severe as what I had experienced in southern Africa.

During my first year in college, I wrote a paper for my English class that surpassed those of my classmates. The professor complimented me for doing such a good job, given the fact that I had come from a non-English-speaking country. One of my fellow students came to me afterwards and asked if my roommate had written the paper for me. He believed that I wasn't capable of writing a good paper and that my white roommate must have at least helped me with it. When I told my roommate about this, he was very upset because he realized that the other student must have thought very poorly of me without cause.

When it comes to police brutality, I haven't been beaten up by police or anything like that, mostly because I value my life and know not to antagonize them. I learned from my Apartheid days that if one talks back to police or resists, that one may be beaten or worse. However, I *have* experienced police harassment. These incidents had nothing to do with any warranted behaviors on my part. I am one of the most passive and non-confrontational people that you will ever meet. The only logical explanation for my experiences of harassment is that of racism.

I have walked into stores and been met with "Can I help you with something?" from the store attendant. If you are a black person and you hear that, you realize that they think you may want to steal something. In one instance, a white person had just entered the same store a moment before me and was never asked the same question.

I have been denied a job position which I was qualified for in favor of a less qualified white person.

I had a father in-law who refused to allow me to marry his daughter because he believed that as a black man, I would be lazy and unable to take care of her. However, after three years of proving him wrong, he changed his view. I didn't stage any protest, all I could do was prove him wrong and not give him any reason to maintain a racist attitude towards me.

I am an American citizen now and have seen and experienced the things that are causing these protests. As a citizen in a country that lets you speak your mind, I want to speak my mind and contribute to a meaningful and lasting solution to this old problem of racism that threatens our prosperity and peace. I hope to use my experience with racism and expertise as a mental health professional to offer suggestions in how to deal with this problem.

I am also the father of a 23 year old college student who has experienced racism in her young life and has expressed her pain along with her friends at peaceful protests. If I can do anything that would alleviate pain from my child's life and make her world a better place, I will move mountains to do so because I love my daughter. I want her to have a good life where she can live in a world better than the one that I have experienced. Books such as this are important resources that can help to inform our community, police and political leaders.

We must end racism and move towards racial equality and harmony. It can be done, but it will take work that must be backed by feasible plans and strategies. We must start with a meaningful dialogue between all the concerned groups of people and the leaders of all relevant racial groups and police organizations. We must also include leaders of all white communities as opposed to discounting them, as they may be the ones who do not realize that there is racism in the country. The starting point of such a dialogue must be a sound understanding of racism.

Chapter 1: Defining the Psychology of Racism

Racism has unique roots that are not necessarily limited to the bad experiences people have had with certain racial groups, although experiences do *reinforce* the pre-existing beliefs about people of other races. It is the pre-existing biases about people of another race that generate racist attitudes and behaviors. The psychology of racism examines the mindset, thoughts and belief systems of racist individuals. I will define racism itself later on in this discussion. Psychology is the study of the human psyche or mind. It is an examination of how the mind functions and influences perception, beliefs and emotions. In this book, we focus on the thought patterns of the racist and how those beliefs lead to racially-based perception and behavior.

When I was studying psychology at the University of North Texas, I read the works of Albert Ellis – a well-known psychologist who lived and practiced in New York City. He developed a theory of psychology that he referred to as *A B C D Theory*. (Ellis 2015) In essence, the theory states that a person's perception of color affects their views and responses. Dr. Ellis would say that a person does not erupt to a bad experience alone; rather it is *belief* concerning an experience that pushes one over the edge. He referred to a bad experience as *A*: the activating event. To illustrate this, I will share the following childhood experience in Africa from my first week in the first grade:

The teacher asked us to write the first four letters of the alphabet. Back then we wrote on the ground with our fingers before we were allowed to write in books. My older siblings had already taught me how to write the whole alphabet, so I thought to myself that I would show off that I could write the whole alphabet (which I did). After finishing, I stood up and motioned to the teacher to come and see my great work that I was so proud of. When the teacher arrived at my station, she saw that I was using my left hand to write. She told me that it was not ok to do that, so she erased my entire work and told me to write only the four letters and, this time, use the finger on the correct (right) hand. I quickly knelt back down, and using my left hand to guide my right finger, I wrote out the entire alphabet. The teacher did not complain.

After school, I went home and my father asked how school went that day. I responded that I had done better than all the students and that I had written the whole alphabet with my normal hand. I told him that the teacher wasn't smart enough to know that I could even use my left hand to write, and that perhaps the school should find a better teacher. My father laughed because he knew that I had totally put my own spin on what otherwise could have been a devastating experience. Dr. Ellis would have said that my **B**elief produced a good **C**onsequence because I **D**isputed the notion that using my left hand was somehow wrong or inferior to using the right hand.

In our brains we have a part that helps us with cognitive processing. When this part of the brain fails to think and process correctly, we can develop some very distorted beliefs that influence how we act and feel about things. This part is called the hippocampus (Van der Kolk, Traumatic Memories 1987). The hippocampus is extremely important because it is the center of our reasoning and memories. This part keeps a record of every experience we have throughout our lives, and whenever we need to remember some of these experiences, it will bring them to our awareness. True racism is embedded there. The good news is that this part of the brain can learn new things, which means that our brain can *un*learn racism and acquire the truth that all men are created equal. We have the ability to learn how to understand other people and accept that others who are different are no worse or better than ourselves. We can get educated if we want to. It's amazing how fast people can learn things when they are motivated. Instead of defunding the police, the police can be taught proper attitudes towards the people they serve. It may even be advantageous if police would be paired with other police partners that come from a race or community that they might be prejudiced against. The same can be said about all people from all walks of life: we can all learn new ways of relating to people who are different from us. Persisting in ignorance about other races only leads to making the wrong assumptions about others.

I have developed the following questions in order to aid in the recognition of ignorance of other races. The manner in which an individual answers these questions can help to reveal how "color-blind" they really are:

1. How often do you converse with individuals of races different from your own?
2. What do you know about their values, beliefs and interests?
3. How many close friends do you have that are from a racial background other than your own?
4. How often have you visited the house of someone of another race to share a meal?
5. How many times have you asked a person from a different country of origin about their culture or customs?
6. Have you ever dated or considered dating a person of another race?
7. If you are a parent, would it ruin your day to discover that your son or daughter is dating a person of another race?
8. How many times have you stopped to help a person of another race?
9. If your boss at work is a person of a different race, do you find yourself having a bad attitude towards them?
10. Do you get upset when you see an interracial couple?
11. Do you find yourself stereotyping people?
12. Do certain skin colors bother you?

13. Do you sometimes make statements about race you wouldn't want some people to hear?
14. Do you sometimes wish all your neighbors were people of your own race?

If you have been paying attention to young people the last two decades, you may realize that they are growing more and more color-blind. They are forming friendships and relationships across all races. I have hope that their generation and the generation after them will experience fewer issues with race than have those of us from older generations. It is also interesting to note that the protesters (especially the young people) are composed of all races, including white people. This just goes to show that our young people are very capable of learning the truth that all men are created equal, which is the heart of racial equality.

What are these deeply held beliefs that produce racism? Each person who holds these beliefs can't help but have racist feelings and attitudes. The most common one is the belief that:

My race is superior to or better than other races.

This belief causes people to look down on people from a different race and despise them without regard to how intelligent, competent, educated or wealthy they may be. Years ago, when I was a doctoral student, my friend Scott and I were mowing lawns in Highland Park. A young lady who lived in the condo where we were working came to give us some water to drink. She proceeded to tell me that if I went back to school and got a college education, I wouldn't have to cut grass for the rest of my life. My friend Scott quickly told the young lady that I was already in school and that I was close to graduating with a PhD. The young lady responded under her breath with these words "But he is still a black man." So to her, the education didn't really matter because only being white mattered, as she was uneducated herself. There is no skin color that is better than the other skin colors, they are just different. The color of one's skin does not determine intelligence or the lack thereof.

Another common belief behind racism is:

Black people are violent and tend to commit crimes more often than white people.

I consider this belief to be behind most incidents of police brutality. The police officer who has such a belief already assumes before he approaches a black man (or sometimes a woman) that he is in danger, and his brain's "fight or flight" modulator kicks into a hyper-alert state (Van der Kolk 1996). Once this happens, the police officer is no longer functioning as an officer but as a survivor fighting for his own life. Even if the person they are approaching is unarmed, their brain is telling them otherwise. On the other side of this equation is the black person who may already be in fear due to the belief that police officers, especially white ones, are either out to use excessive force or deal harshly with them. Worse still, there may be fear that the officer is going to kill them even if the officer is just checking for something minor. Because of the "fight or flight" response, the black person may also run or fight back, which might result in being killed by the officer. There are many explanations for these types of escalations on both sides, but the truth is that deeply-held beliefs on both sides must change. Some claim that statistics prove that black people commit more crimes than white people. However, statistics do not explain *why* there is such an imbalance when it comes to crime/race ratios. Let's say there are two guys driving down the road, one black and one white, and both are driving over the speed limit. It is actually more likely that the black person would be pulled over and the white one would not. Therefore, the black man becomes part of an inaccurate statistic.

Another deeply held belief is:

When a black man is driving in a white neighborhood, he is scoping the area for a planned robbery.

Years ago when I was still a doctoral student, I was driving my old (but decent) little car going to visit a very good friend of mine in the Highland Park Village shopping center. I was pulled over simply because my car and my race seemed out of place in that community. I wasn't speeding or doing anything questionable. When I was asked what I was doing there, I told the officer that I was visiting a good friend of mine, whom I named. I could see that the officer didn't believe me. My friend was a rich white businessman, and the officers couldn't believe he could have a poor black guy as his friend. They followed me to my friend's upscale store, and when we got there they went inside to ask him if he knew me. Thankfully, my friend told the officer that not only were we good friends, but that we went to the same church in that neighborhood. He told them that I was also an Olympic runner and PhD candidate. My friend made certain that they shouldn't worry about me being in that neighborhood. That saved me, as the officers already had a false preconception that I did not belong there.

I have also heard another explanation for such a policing attitude which is the belief that:

> The police have experienced so many black people engaged in certain types of crimes that they are justified in predicting that black people are prone to do such things.

The problem with this is that past experiences are not the best predictors. There is always the possibility that new experiences will not conform to old ones. I believe it is not the experiences, but rather their interpretations that leads to such a conclusions. It is these deeply held beliefs that spur some police officers to do what was done to George Floyd and others.

I am sure there are many police officers that are not racist and do their job well. This is why I don't believe that calling to defund the police is the answer to ending racism. We need to end racism and not end law and order. No civil society ever survived without law and order. If you don't believe me, observe those countries where law and order has totally broken down. I don't think that the people who are calling to defund the police are truly thinking of what would ensue if there were no police in the streets. I think this sentiment is coming from a great deal of pain and hurt that has lasted for such a long time. When people are grieving, emotions can run very high, and it is not the time to formulate policy. As a mental health professional who has spent most of his life studying and helping people deal with their emotions and minds, I know when to bring up topics of change and when to listen to heightened emotions. Even though I do not dismiss my client's emotions, I know that it is only when those emotions come down that we can rationally discuss change. In the present political situation, those cities who are actually defunding the police are making a huge mistake because they will soon find out that racism will persist and that crime will increase. With no law and order, they will regret their decisions. On the other hand, I agree with those cities that are working to change certain aspects of policing behavior and policies, as that is part of educating the police. My point in this book is that racism isn't a problem that lies only with the police – it is also a *societal* issue. Racism is found within both society and some police officers, and both contribute to police brutality. It is a step in the right direction to outlaw police brutality and racial profiling, but these actions alone will not eliminate racism.

Chapter 2: Defining Racism

What is racism? What makes a person a racist? Is racism a problem found only in white people? Does the color of one's skin automatically make them a racist? Are racist persons *aware* that they are in fact racist? Are people born racist? Can people hold racist beliefs about their *own* race? Is "white privilege" racism? These questions are of the utmost importance in our quest to better understand racism. Therefore, we must consider each of these questions and seek to answer them. By engaging in this process, we can progress towards a solution to this ongoing problem that has caused so much pain in the world.

We will begin by defining what racism is:

Racism is the belief and practice of seeing and treating people of a different race negatively simply because of their race.

Racism is the assumption that one's own race is the best and that other races are not as good, or even wrong, bad or evil. Racism is the focus on negative aspects of a race other than one's own. The racist always views one's own race as having the answers to the problems of the world, whereas other races are seen as inferior and not deserving of the same opportunities.

As an example, white people went to Africa as they were exploring beyond their white world and encountered different people with different ways of living. They also discovered valuable minerals such as gold and diamonds. They learned that the inhabitants of Africa had different customs and varying kinds of factual knowledge. Gradually, white people began to settle in Africa and establish communities for themselves that mirrored those of their homelands. Before long, they began to establish a system of rule over Africa that ignored the fact that African peoples already had their own systems of government. White people assumed their way of government was better. Terms such as "savages," "primitive" and other terms (which I won't mention) became popular descriptors for the indigenous populations of Africa.

After a time, the African people realized that they were being robbed of both their ways of life and material resources. It likely would have been acceptable if the white people came to *share* in the natural riches instead of exploiting the people. Overtime, white people took over the whole continent of Africa and established themselves as superior in all aspects. Don't get me wrong —white people brought civilization to Africa, but bringing new information and knowledge doesn't make one group of people superior and another inferior. This same sad racial injustice was imposed on the Native Americans here in the United States and Canada and on the aboriginal groups of Australia. In all of these situations, the indigenous peoples of these lands suffered, and in some cases *still* suffer, racial injustices and discrimination – the products of racism.

We are all aware of what Hitler did to one group of people who were from non-German backgrounds. He tortured and murdered millions of Jewish people simply because they were Jewish. Even to this day, Jewish people around the world still suffer from racism. Some people who hate them don't even know why they do so. Hitler's racism persists to this day in the form of white supremacism and groups such as the KKK. Racism is a very dangerous poison of the mind – when takes hold, rationality departs from the minds of those consumed by it. Nobody is born a racist; racism is learned. Sometimes it is learned by example. While some racist parents may not sit their kids down and tell them how bad certain races are, their example of treating others poorly serves to teach a child racist behaviors. One can easily observe that small children play with other children without any consideration given to race. However, when a parent tells the child to stop such play, even though the child may not understand why, the child will begin to develop racist attitudes without conscious awareness.

Modeling by example is a powerful teaching tool for both positive and negative lessons. Parents can model racial equality and harmony or they can model racism. I remember many years ago, when I still lived in Africa, I had a missionary friend – the reverend Tom Jackson (who, along with his wife Lois, is still serving God in Africa). I was in their house countless times and viewed it as a second home. I was welcomed there even though I was a black person. Their oldest son, Matthew, even called me "Uncle Jerry." Each time I would leave their house to go to my house in the ghetto, the little boy would cry because he wanted to go with his Uncle. Many years later, he wanted to make sure that his uncle would be at his wedding. At the wedding, I recall seeing myself present in many of the slideshow photos, like another family member. The members of the Jackson family did not have a racist bone in their bodies. Even to this very day, Rev. Tom Jackson and his wife are known throughout Zimbabwe for their color blind reputation.

Is racism a problem that affects only white people? Certainly not, as racist views can be found in individuals of all races. Many years ago, I was having coffee at a McDonalds in Springdale, Arkansas. I have referred to this place as my second home for over forty years because my adoptive family (Joe and Charlotte Layman) lives there. I was a college student having coffee on break with a white girl from my college. She was just a friend, but two black girls came by and gave me the biggest stares and evil looks. This confused me because I was expecting these sisters to be very friendly towards me in a town that was almost all white. One of the girls was brave enough to come up to me and call me "uncle Tom." Back then, I didn't know much about American colloquialisms, so I wondered why she would call me her uncle but give me dirty looks (and my name wasn't Tom). My friend from college saw that I was perplexed and tried to help me understand what was happening. She told me that those girls were very upset with me for fraternizing with white people. So the "uncle Tom" reference was a form of *black* racism. On the other hand, I have learned that white people who are friendly with black people are sometimes are called "nigger lovers" by other whites.

Name-calling is never a mature or constructive way of dealing with people because it promotes very unhealthy views of others, further fanning the flames of racism. Black racism is no better than white racism. Racism is racism.

I recall watching a group of young black guys playing a pick-up game of basketball in a park as I was passing by on my run. Two white guys were talking to the group and I could tell that one black guy wasn't happy by his gesturing. I stopped and asked what was going on. The black guy told me that he was opposed to these two white guys trying to play with them. I asked the guy why it wasn't ok for the two white guys to play with them. His answer almost shocked me. He said that the two white guys would not be good enough to compete with them. He told me in a joking fashion that "white men can't jump." I then suggested that they try these guys and see if they truly couldn't jump. What I wanted to accomplish was convincing the black guys to allow the white guys to play with them. I am not a basketball player – otherwise I would have volunteered to play with them as well. The young black guys, out of respect for me as an older black man, allowed the white guys to play. What followed was very interesting. The two white guys were far better players than expected and the black guys started giving the white guys high fives! Right there we broke racism from the black side.

Black racism towards white people is just as bad. When those of us in the black community place all white people in one category and say *they* are all racist, we commit the same sin we condemn them for. Some of us may think that we are just giving white people a taste of their own medicine. We shouldn't forget that two wrongs don't make a right. Name-calling (such as calling white police officers "pigs") doesn't help. When one does that, one brings oneself to down to a level that provokes retaliation. There are even cases of black people discriminating against other black people on the basis of skin color. Some black people who are much darker than others sometimes see themselves as "truly" black and view others with lighter skin as "less." This, too, is black racism. Not all people with racism beliefs and practices *know* that they are racists. Most people do not want to be seen as a racist due to the negative connotations of the term. Some may not realize that they have racist beliefs until being confronted with a situation that brings out their racism.

Years ago, when I was working in a psychiatric hospital, one of my nurses reported to me that an item was missing from the unit in which I was the director. She proceeded to tell me that there were several black mental health techs, and she was certain that one of them had taken the item. When I asked her how she was so sure, she assured me that young black men are good at stealing because they have a lot of experience with it in their communities. Before I could decide how to deal with the situation, the poor guys had been interrogated, only for the hospital to discover that the item had been misplaced by the night shift nurses. One of the young black techs complained about this and pointed out to the nurse that she was a racist, which she strongly denied. There are many people like that nurse who are not even aware that they hold racist beliefs until a situation arises and it comes out.

We can ask ourselves the following questions to help further discover racist tendencies:

1. Do you automatically feel uneasy around a person of a different race?
2. Do you find it hard to trust a person of a different race?
3. Do you find it hard to relate to a neighbor of a different race?
4. Do you often tell racial jokes without realizing that it may be offensive to people of other races?
5. Do you dislike someone simply because of their race?
6. Do you wish the world was full of people of only your own race?

7. Do you think that only people from your own race are beautiful or handsome?
8. Do you find it unacceptable to worship with persons of a different race?
9. If your congregation has members of a different race, how many of those people are in leadership positions?
10. Do you discourage your young children from playing with kids of a different race?

If we are serious about ending racism, it would be helpful for us to search our souls continuously. It is easy to protest and counter-protest, but introspection is more difficult. The path that I am proposing to overcome racism will not be an easy one. Everyone must do their part. We can't just ask white people to change their attitudes and ignore the racist attitudes of others.

Many don't consider the fact that one can have racist beliefs and attitudes towards their own race, but this is a problem as well. I once listened to a conversation between two Hispanic guys and quickly the conversation turned very negative. One guy called the other a "wetback" and other names that I didn't recognize because I am not familiar with that culture and language. Then another Hispanic guy came to the rescue and asked the guys to treat each other kindly, as they had enough problems from ill treatment by white people. Even though this admonition did not address the core issue, the guy recognized the expression of racist sentiments against one's own group.

I understand that people may sometimes internalize racist attitudes they encounter from those who mistreat them, but this mechanism only fuels the fire of racism. When a black woman says to herself "I know I'm not as beautiful as that white girl," she is actually putting herself down. It may be true that some black guy may have left her for a white girl, but there is no reason to internalize that. The same internalization can also result when a white guy states that a black guy who is dating a white girl is trying to "conquer the white race" or "prove something." The black guy should not become defensive if he is truly motivated by love and compatibility. When we accept the racist narratives of others, we subjugate ourselves to constant vigilance and unease. This, too, empowers the racist.

Being white doesn't automatically make someone a racist, nor does *disagreeing* with a person of a different race. Disliking bad behavior doesn't make anyone a racist, nor does criticizing minority politicians when criticism is *warranted*. People are born with the race they inherit, and there is nothing they can do about it. No one has to apologize for being white, black or brown. During the George Floyd protests, I saw some white people apologizing for what they called "white privilege." I am not sure what motivates this, but being white or black are not crimes. So what is true white privilege? It cannot be equated with being born white; it is the status of white people that is elevated above that of other races due to the advantages that are granted to white people.

Once, a white friend of mine walked into a bank here to apply for a business loan that was much larger than a loan that I had applied for only hours prior. Due to white privilege, his application was accepted and the loan was granted, whereas I was told that I needed to go to a bank that would consider an SBA loan (which I had not asked for). My friend benefited from white privilege, but he could not be held responsible for the fact that I was denied – so why should he have to apologize for being white? It is true that white privilege results from racist thinking, and that the beneficiary cannot be held responsible unless such a person thinks that they are deserve it.

Racism is not directed against only black and brown people. It can target anyone: members of minority or majority populations and even people in power. While often not at the forefront of race dialogue, people of Asian descent are often subjected to racism as well. I recall talking to a group of young white guys at a motorcycle shop. We were discussing different models of motorcycles. I was attempting to describe a certain kind of sports bike that I see a lot of young men riding. As I was talking, a young Asian guy rode into the shop on one of those bikes. One of the guys I was talking to pointed to the bike to me and asked if that was the one, which I affirmed. Then the young white guy told me that it was a "rice burner." I was confused at the time because I knew that motorcycles did not run on rice, but I later learned that was a reference to a stereotype about Asians. The guys thought it was funny, but I doubt that the Asian guy felt that way. If we are going to make any progress in getting rid of racism, we must apply some serious effort towards learning what kinds of statements those of others races may deem to be offensive. Racism tends to numb or deaden one's conscience to the point that one is no longer bothered by something that should not be tolerated.

On the news today I saw a photo of some Democratic senators kneeling and wearing what appeared to me as some style of African clothing. Anyone who saw that can only assume that this was meant to represent solidarity with black people during the protests. I personally was offended by it because such action will not help to diminish racism one bit. The problem goes much deeper than clothes. Wearing a particular form of clothing does not identify one as an African-American. How can white people identify with us by wearing a certain style of "our" clothes, which the majority of us don't wear or have never worn? We seek equal treatment and justice and the elimination of racism. We desire to see meaningful dialogue between all of the leaders who are involved in enacting the much needed changes in our country. These leaders should include members of all groups that are affected by racial tensions.

This issue has boiled to the surface during an election year, and as a result of this unfortunate timing, our politicians are milking it for all its worth. They are focused on winning the elections to maintain power and preserve the status quo. Why should we believe that our politicians would suddenly have an epiphany that racism is wrong when they have stood by watching all these years and taken little action? It is also unfortunate that the media is also exploiting the unrest to the fullest at the behest of their own partisan agendas. They often manipulate the coverage to portray their preferred party in a favorable light while demonizing the opposition. Due to this, mainstream media has lost credibility and is no longer trusted by many people.

Chapter 3: The Dangers of Racism

Some people hold the view that the concurrent looting and vandalism that has been seen during the protests is not connected to the issue of racism. It is my view that it is all connected, but this will be discussed in greater detail later. First, we will discuss some of the most obvious and dangerous consequences of racism in the global sphere. Throughout history, people have been killed simply because they were different in some way from those in power. We have all heard of ethnic cleansings. Many innocent people have lost their lives simply because they belonged to a different religion or were of a different race.

Among the chants of the ongoing protests are the names of black people who have died at the hands of police. There is a strong sentiment that even one person dying at the hands of a police officer is one too many. Lives have been lost because of this issue. On the other hand, police officers have also died during the protests, and that, too, is unacceptable. If racism wasn't an issue, things would be very different. Lives – *all lives* – really matter, and no one should be dying in senseless violence.

Racism also has also proved costly to societies in many other ways. Some groups have segregated themselves into enclaves where they feel comfortable being around others of their own race. Some say that this has nothing to do with racism, but I beg to differ. If race had nothing to do with this phenomena, we wouldn't have these separated communities. They were born out of racism. In a truly color-blind society, people would not feel the desire to associate only with those of their own race. While it may feel more natural and comfortable to live in a homogenous community, it limits interaction with, and understanding of others, who are different. When I was a doctoral student, I had a classmate who, like myself, was from Zimbabwe. We frequently talked, and one day I suggested that we should also try to get to know students from other countries as well, which would mutually facilitate better understanding. Sure enough, as we spent more time with a more diverse crowd, the more our lives were enriched by their different perspectives and experiences.

Racism can also results in the reduction of the opportunities to interact with and learn from different people. This kind of learning cannot take place in a classroom. Ignorance isn't as harmless many might assume. It is the ignorance of other races that causes some police officers to treat certain racial groups differently from their own. As I watched the Minneapolis police chief speaking at the center of a large crowd of protesters, I wondered if anyone understood why his message had such resonance. It is true that being a person of color served as a bridge between him and the community. Yes, he shared the racial roots of the man who was killed by the white police officer, which enabled the chief to identify with the pain. But the biggest factor in his break-through with the crowd lay in the fact that he had learned how to approach black people. He took off his hat when addressing the family of George Floyd, which the protesters immediately recognized as a sign of respect. The chief had learned through his years of policing in the black community how to relate. I believe that if he had been white but behaved in the same way, he most likely would also have experienced the same response. What I am talking about transcends race, anyone from any race can learn how to approach people of other races. I have seen police officers treat suspects with respect. Those police officers are well trained. As a mental health professional, I sometimes have to call 911 when I have an emergency with a client who is out of control. I have been impressed with those officers who have been trained to deescalate situations involving people with mental problems. The officers have been very respectful towards both my clients and myself. We have all heard of cases where police officers have shot and killed a mentally ill patient on the street because they lacked the training to know what approach to take when dealing with such a person.

Psychological screening and training for police officers is also of great importance. Policing can be challenging and traumatic, and officers with prior trauma or other deep psychological issues should not be allowed to join the police force. Psychological maladjustments will one day surface as they try to deal with the stress of perceived danger. Officers that are engulfed by fear should not be approaching people that they believe may kill them. Even when there is no indication that a suspect is dangerous, the judgment of an officer with psychological issues can be seriously impaired.

Police are people, too. I have friends that are police officers. I have taught graduate courses to students who went on to enter the police force. I have had neighbors who were police officers. I have gone to church with people who were police officers. I have had clients who were police officers. It is not true that all of them are racists or practitioners of police brutality. Generalization is also a form of discrimination that only fans the flames of racism.

The polarization of the media is exasperating the problem by often painting a picture that racism is endemic in law enforcement, and that police are at the root of most of society's problems. The bias of the mainstream media is fomenting an inaccurate view of policing throughout the world. I am very disappointed by the media, which has abandoned the unbiased reporting of news. Some news anchors go on rants about what they think should be happening as if they are politicians. They are poisoning people's minds and should be called out on this.

I have worked with military service members in hospital settings as the director of the *Post-Traumatic Stress Disorder Program* and was responsible for determining the fitness of service members for redeployment. Those who are not fit are assigned to a desk job or similar duties as designated by the military. This action is spurred by the mandate to prevent a soldier from endangering others that he or she are serving alongside. The military also wants to ensure the well-being of its people. Our military serves us, and its members should be adequately cared for, even if it means hospitalization or therapy. The police force should be doing something similar. If I could psychologically test some of the officers who commit acts of pathology on our streets, I suspect that I would find deep pathological problems. Pathology does not mean that one is a terrible person; rather, it indicates that a person needs help and should be withdrawn from a work situation until they have recovered.

We must keep in mind that not all police officers around the globe killed George Floyd, and they shouldn't have to pay for the crime of those who did. We must not forget that police officer is someone's husband, wife, dad, mom or child. Their families want to see them come home. Also, some officers are truly worthy of their jobs. While we are justified in expressing anger when a racist proclaims that all blacks are violent or lazy, we should also empathize with good police officers when someone says that they are all bad.

Racism has cost societies the loss of great potential talent. Due to their racial background, many people have been excluded from certain professions or positions. Not long ago, my family and I saw a movie about a black doctor who took a position in a rural white community. The people in that community refused to let him treat them because he was black. Finally, a white woman was about to give birth and the black man was the only doctor available. He delivered her baby, which opened the eyes of the other people to see that a doctor is a doctor regardless of race. Only racism equates race with competency.

When I was a young teenager, I worked with my brother picking cotton on a white-owned farm. My brother was the supervisor – he was good at his job and knew a lot about how to grow, pick, pack and sell cotton. The owner then hired a young white man who didn't know anything about cotton. He failed miserably, and the owner ended up bringing my brother back to run the operation after finally realizing that being white doesn't make one smart or able. The owner of the farm lost money because of his racist ignorance that prompted him to replace a competent black man with an incompetent and inexperienced white man.

Racism causes societies to overlook and marginalize certain groups within their populations. In South Africa's Apartheid system, the white government placed all the well-constructed buildings, stores and other structures only in white areas. The wants and needs of the black people were ignored because we were seen as non-essential except as a manual labor force. Even at that time, there were countless bright, young black people who had attained very high levels of education overseas in America, England, or Germany. When they returned to Zimbabwe, they were denied jobs that they were qualified for, solely on the account of being black. I remember that one of these educated men attempted to purchase a nice house in a "white suburb," but failed to do so because of racism. Years later, after much societal change, the man revealed to me and my colleagues that he was told that he couldn't buy the house that he wanted because he couldn't afford it. In actuality, he had the money. I am sure that similar things have frequently occurred elsewhere in the world.

Some Americans are puzzled by the fact that these protests are happening in other distant countries. However, this should not come as a surprise, as the issue is much bigger than the killing of George Floyd. There are many, many George Floyds around the globe because of racism. It is also important to note that racism not only kills individuals but also destroys many other aspects of people's lives, such as dignity. Can you imagine how it must feel to be treated as less than human by someone that you know is no better than you? Can you imagine how it must feel to be passed by for a job or promotion because of the color of your skin? Can you imagine how it must feel to be innocent and then arrested, tried, convicted, and imprisoned for years only to find that you were presumed guilty due to the color of your skin? These are some of the costs of racism for those of us who are subjected to it.

We must also not forget that there are forms of bigotry that take racism to the extreme, such as the KKK and other white supremacist groups. Many fear the potential for backlash to the current protests from such groups due to the violence that they have historically perpetuated. Failure to deal with the current protests effectively and amicably could unleash a tide of pro-white counter-protests that could perpetuate the cycle of violence and unrest that would move the country even further from peace. The world is already in a great deal of turmoil and can't take much more. I understand *why* people protest with intense emotion, but violence is not a necessity to make one's voice heard.

Chapter 4: The Psychology of Protest

As a young person growing up in southern Africa, I heard the stories of Nelson Mandela, who was imprisoned in South Africa for protesting the Apartheid system. The system was evil and intolerable to black people. I heard about the police brutality towards black people in South Africa. Even though I had never been to South Africa and it was not my country, my heart and emotions were with the people of South Africa because I could identify with them. Mr. Mandela was arrested for protesting government policy, but he did so in a peaceful fashion. Protesting simply was not permitted in that part of the world.

The black people in South Africa were not only there long before Europeans arrived, but they also were the majority population. In spite of these facts, they were terribly oppressed and had every right to protest their treatment. All cries and requests for systemic change were denied and totally ignored, leaving black people with few options to be heard. They were forced to make a decision between resigning themselves to lives of misery or doing something about it.

A leader rose up – the lawyer Nelson Mandela. It was his study of the law that helped him to realize that he and the people of South Africa should have certain rights. He led his people to protest this injustice with a clear message. Even while in prison, Mr. Mandela led the protest because of his conviction that his message was clear and valid. After 27 years of peaceful protests, the white government of South Africa ended the racist system of government. However, it did not result in the expulsion of all racists from the country, and I am sure that there are some individuals who still feel superior to other people. In some cases reverse discrimination is just as bad.

The events that led to Mr. Mandela becoming the president of South Africa were brought about by meaningful dialogue. Mandela is remembered for holding *Truth and Reconciliation* meetings throughout the country to heal the wounds of racism. Here in our country, we need the likes of President Mandela to lead us in meaningful dialogue between government leaders and communities that are affected by racism. Those involved must be cool and collected if this is going to work, as tempers and ugly rhetoric will only escalate the situation.

I recall listening to the news on the radio one morning during the period of Apartheid. A young man named Stephen Bhiko was a civil right activist protesting the same injustices that Mr. Mandela was protesting. Stephen Bhiko had been arrested and imprisoned, where he was beaten to death by white prison guards. As with the death of George Floyd, this event caused a great deal of pain to the people of South Africa and Zimbabwe. As a young teenager I felt pain and helplessness, too, because there didn't seem to be anything that would happen to change things. In spite of all setbacks though, Mr. Mandela continued on with his protest. So what was he saying in his protest? He wasn't able to go out and walk in the streets with signs, throw rocks and bottles at police, burn buildings, torch police cars or loot any stores. He was in prison. His message resonated because it was nonviolent.

In the same vein as Mandela, Dr. Martin Luther King brought change to the US through peaceful protest. We should not discount what Dr. King did for us in this country and the world through his example of inspiration and encouragement. We celebrate a holiday in his memory because we recognize the importance of what he was fighting for. Many protests have something in common – the desire for concrete change. In Dr. King's *I Have a Dream* speech, he clearly articulates his goals. Dr. King was a very passionate man, but he did not allow himself to be controlled by emotion. He was a reasonable man facing unreasonable racism. His activism cost him his life, but the movement prevailed in the end.

People protest when their voices have been ignored for too long.

The most effective protests are those that are peaceful and well-organized, as they bring together opposing parties to engage in meaningful dialogue. Protests have erupted around the world due to severe disagreements, and those that end in meaningful dialogue often bear good fruit. On the other hand, protests that are motivated chiefly by revenge only increase the violence. Both Mr. Mandela and Dr. King had their visions set on the greater prizes of lasting change and freedom. Today, we must align our protest with values such as theirs. Otherwise, we will face counter-protests and a vicious cycle of enduring pain.

Protests have taken many different forms throughout the history of the world. Growing up in Zimbabwe, I listened to the protest songs of a musician by the name of Thomas Mapfumo, who is still creating music protesting the kinds of oppression that found today. Rather than resort to violence, he used his voice to send a subtle message that was heard loud and clear by the racist government, which harassed him. In Jamaica, Bob Marley used his voice to protest the racial injustices that black people everywhere experienced. I remember attending a celebration of Zimbabwe'sj independence in the capital city of Harare where Bob Marley was singing his protest music. He continued to protest until he died because he believed that racial equality had not yet been fully realized.

It would be a mistake to fail to acknowledge the changes that have taken place since the days of slavery and segregation in this country and around the world. We have come a long way, which is why I believe that we can do even better. To continue to progress though, we must keep working. No one would ever say that Dr. King died in vain, or that Mr. Mandela suffered for nothing. I want to make sure that the death of Mr. George Floyd will also not be in vain. So far, his death has resulted in a movement bigger than anything seen in the past and has touched people around the globe. We must strive to ensure that his death contributes to the end of racism.

Some people have protested silently by staging sit-ins at work or other places where they want to send a message of the need for change, *concrete* change. Whenever significant change has been the outcome of a protest, there has been meaningful dialogue among the people involved. I truly respect some of the messages I have seen from different people speaking up about the problems of racism and injustice. I have heard some politicians talk about what they will do to change things and bring about racial justice and equality. What I haven't heard the politicians say is just how they will go about doing this. I haven't heard them specify which members of the community will be brought into the discussion. I also haven't heard much talk about having meaningful dialogue with the leadership of law enforcement in the country. Abolishing the police without having a meaningful discussion deprives society one side of the debate. I have already mentioned that abolishing the police is not a wise decision. If this were to happen, we would be the first progressive nation to regress, as a country cannot function in the absence of law and order.

We must now discuss the way in which peaceful protests, violence, and looting are intertwined. First of all, let me assure you that I do not agree with any type of violent protests, let alone looting and the destruction of property such as burning police cars and precincts. However, there are reasons why these things happen in the midst of an otherwise peaceful protest. I have already mentioned how protests have a tendency to evoke strong emotions in people. Some people have very poor impulse control, and during such times of heightened negative emotions, people tend to lose control. When that happens, people can express their anger in destructive ways. People with poor impulse control don't need much provocation for them to explode. Of course, that doesn't *justify* their actions, but it does help to explain them. It may not always be true that groups engaged in violence and groups protesting peacefully are mutually exclusive. Some people can react in different ways at different times. However, those who loot or resort to violence overshadow and diminish the valid causes of protest.

Some people seem confused when observing the diversity of the individuals who are protesting racial injustice. We have seen white people and even law enforcement join in protests against police brutality. However, this should not come as a surprise to anyone who wants justice and finds the killing of George Floyd and racist behavior to be unacceptable. Good people will always stand up to defend those who are mistreated without regard to race or societal position.

I have noticed that the majority of these protesters tend to be young people of all races. I have already pointed out that our young people tend to be more color-blind than those of us who are older. Our young people are more likely to have interracial friendships and romantic relationships. As a result, they tend to know more about people of different races because of their frequent interactions. Some of them even go out of their way to try and relate to people of other races because they value diversity and knowledge.

I have also noticed that people who have lived abroad and experienced other cultures tend to be more accepting of people of different races. This is true of myself, as my international travels have provided me with opportunities to spend quality time with people from many different countries. I have formed friendships and relationships with people different from me. I don't feel any need to restrict my circle of friends to those like myself. I remember being asked by a good friend why I didn't go to a black church instead of the predominately white one that I was attending at that time. My response was that I was going to the church that was in my community and that I wasn't going to drive 30 miles when there was a good church a couple miles away from my house. It did not bother me one bit if I was going to be the only black person there. I was the only black person in the professional organization that I belonged to for many years before other black people joined. I told my friend that I didn't believe that worshiping God limited us to worshiping only with people of our own race. I believe that all

Christians belong to one race and one nation in Christ. This naturally brings me to talking about racism in the church.

Chapter 5: Racism in the Church

By "church," I mean all churches as opposed to a particular denomination. Christians refer to this as the *universal* church or body of Christ that is composed of believers from every nation and culture around the globe. Obviously, distance, language, and culture do influence *how* people worship God which is the one of the primary reasons that different nationalities have their own variations on the concept of church. I want to make sure that no one thinks that I am denying that there is a valid reason for the existence of different forms of worship and denominations. When I refer to racism in the church, I am talking about the unnecessary exclusion of people from a church due to their race.

If a white person wishes to go to a black church due to preference for the style of preaching or music, or because they have friends that attend, they should be able to do so without being ostracized by the members of the congregation, who worship the same God and speak the same language. What reason besides racism could be given to deny the fellowship of believers to individuals of a race other than one's own?

When I lived in Africa, I was a pastor of a black church in the black township. On the other side of town there were several white churches. The white church members gathered on Friday nights at a Christian coffee house in the town center for fellowship and evangelism. I was friends with a white American missionary lady, and one day she invited me to accompany her to the coffeehouse. When we got to the door, I was told I that I could not enter. My white friend asked why, and when one man said that it was for white people only, she protested that she didn't see any sign and that it was not in keeping with Christian values. With her protest, I was let in. The guy who tried to prevent my admission was motivated by racism, as there was no legitimate reason to refuse me entry.

These days, I doubt that most churches in first-world countries would blatantly discriminate as in my experience. The racism in our churches today tends to be very subtle, and most of the people who still have racist attitudes and beliefs may not be aware of it. Here are some more questions to help identify racist tendencies:

1. If your church is multiethnic, how many of your elders are from different races?
2. If your church is predominantly of one race, what are you doing to attract people of different races in your area?
3. If you have members of your church who are from different races, have you befriended or invited any of them to your house?
4. If your church is predominantly of one race, how often are guest speakers of another race invited?
5. In your church how many times have you heard a sermon against racism?
6. Does your preacher or other leaders say negative things about people of different races?
7. How much interaction have your children had with people of different races?
8. Do you ever think that your race is actually better than other races?
9. Do you hold onto any stereotypes about people of different races?
10. How often do you pray for people of other races when you are made aware of their plight?

The answers to the above questions should indicate whether you need to work more on becoming color-blind. The Church should lead the way in modeling color-blindness, as Christians have benefitted the most from the color-blindness of Jesus Christ, God's only Son whose love for the world transcends all color, race and culture. He left His throne in Heaven and came down to earth in the form of a helpless human baby even though He was God. You can't get any more non-racist than that. As the Apostle Paul put it in Philippians 2:5-8:

"In your relationships with one another, have the same mindset as Christ Jesus: Who being in very nature God, did not consider equality with God something to be used to his own advantage; rather he made himself nothing by taking the very nature of a servant, being made in human likeness and being found in appearance as a man he humbled himself by becoming obedient to death even death on a cross."

What does that tell us as Christians about treating others? We can simply say that Christianity requires that we should set an example of color-blindness and never practice any form of racism.

I happen to go to a church that is predominantly white with a white pastor, even though I am a black person. I have been very impressed with the color-blindness of the pastor. The church is very large, so while I have not personally met him, if he were to talk with me, I would expect that he would treat me no differently than the other members of the congregation. The leadership of the church is composed of people from many different ethnic backgrounds. In this church, one's race does not factor into either preferential or discriminatory treatment. The pastor's own daughter is married to a black man.

When I attend this church, racial differences disappear in the Body of Christ. However, this has not been true of all of my church experiences. Years ago, I remember realizing that my church was insensitive to me as a black person when the church did nothing after hearing of my loss of family members back in Africa. I received no condolences from the pastor or leaders of the church. There were no cards or visits when I returned from 8 funerals. I watched as the church gave flowers, cards and meals to other families that were either ill or lost someone. The only reason for this that I could think of was that the white lives that the church knew mattered more than the black lives in Africa that they didn't know. But they did knew me, as I was a member. While the members of the church were otherwise very good and caring people, they probably didn't see anything wrong with their lack of action. Situations like this are very common in Churches around the world.

When I first came to America, I heard that there was a Christian university that did not permit interracial dating, which I was told was prohibited by scripture. If you asked the people at that university if they were racist, I'm sure that they would have denied it. They would not have stopped to think about how such a policy impacted people. They would have been unconcerned with what messages they were sending to the world about race and God's view of humanity. How could the same people read parts of the Bible that calls on people of all nations, all tribes and all languages yet not consider that perhaps God is all inclusive and he no respecter of persons? The Bible specifically says that in Christ there is neither Jew nor Gentile and neither male nor female. According to the apostle Paul, the Church is God's agent on earth and should be the expression and manifestation of His mystery of redemption that includes all people. In a way, racism in the church may be worse than anywhere else. When the church fails to accurately portray the mystery of God, it fails God.

Jesus was aware of the racist beliefs and attitudes that the teachers of the Jewish Law held towards gentiles in general, and the Samaritans in particular. Jesus approached a Samaritan woman and asked her for a drink of water. The woman was shocked because she knew that Jews had no dealings with either Samaritans or women like herself. At the time, tradition even dictated that any Jewish person who passed through Samaria would have to engage in ceremonial washing as Samaritans were considered unclean. Jesus was fully aware that according to culture and tradition that he wasn't supposed to talk to her, but he did so anyway. Jesus socialized with everyone and embraced them. There should be no room for racism in the hearts of those that claim to follow him.

It will be interesting to how churches respond to the protests. Will the church be a voice in the move towards healing a divided country? I truly hope that the church leads by example. It is the church that can show our society that it is possible for people of different races to live together in harmony. The Christian church in America has a long history of sending missionaries to other lands to reach people of many races with the Gospel. In order to do this, they had to bridge racial and cultural divides. Missionaries who immersed themselves in the lives of the natives were more successful than those who practiced segregation. I believe that the act of bridging the gap demonstrated the love of the missionaries and won many to Christ. Today we need the church to be the missionaries to a world plagued by racism. We must do more than preaching – we must live out the love of Christ in the way that we treat others.

Chapter 6: Racism and Politics

The focus of politics should be the governance of society. Politicians are chosen by the people to enact laws. In a multiethnic society such as that of the United States of America, it is critical that our politicians mirror our diversity to ensure that all people are represented. The political climate of our nation in its early days was marred by blatant racism, slavery, and discrimination. As a nation, we have come a long way but have not yet fully achieved racial equality and justice for all.

In history, some political figures who publicly held racist beliefs were confronted. Some felt compelled to change their views in order to win elections. I have watched the reactions of our politicians during these protests to see if they understand the underlying issues. I haven't heard any politicians approve of the police brutality that took George Floyd's life, and I think that both Democrats and Republicans recognize that there is a problem. However, politicians have been less clear on how to remedy the situation. Already, some are talking about changing certain laws, which sounds reasonable and promising. Whatever course of action is taken, it must be swift to stem the tide of the protests.

However, I am also concerned about an overly rushed political response that may not put enough thought and work into finding lasting solutions. It is clear that the problem goes deeper than issues of policing. What happened to George Floyd and others before him has been going on for a long time. It is very clear that police reform is only one of the protesters demands, but I am afraid that much of the message has been drowned out by the focus on police. I have said from the beginning in this book that racism is an underlying cause of police brutality and other related issues. We cannot resolve the issue of police brutality without resolving racism. I have also repeatedly called for a meaningful dialogue between the key people that need to be involved in order to address this adequately. It is not enough for the politicians to come up with solutions apart from the people. Community and police leaders, educators and mental health experts must be included. Perhaps even the makers of police-themed television shows should become involved in the dialogue. The solution to the crisis will not be easily solved, and it would be a mistake to think otherwise.

I am fully aware that as a nation, we can be a very impatient people. We demand quick fixes to complicated problems. Health experts warned over and over again that the Coronavirus Pandemic is not over yet, but many people are now behaving as if everything is fine. As we ignore reality, the rate of infections, hospitalizations and deaths continues to climb. We behave as if there is no virus simply because we can't wait for lasting solutions. I am afraid we will respond to the protests in the same way. In such a scenario, the protests (or worse) will certainly engulf us again in the near future.

It is unfortunate that the protests are occurring during an election year when our politicians are focused on votes. Some are even exploiting these protests for their own political purposes. If siding with the protesters seems to be the winning move, then for them that is the card to play. Once in power though, many politicians seem to forget why the people elected them. This happens year after year and yet people seem to ignore it. I am afraid that if our politicians backpedal on the issue of racism that there will be more trouble down the road. In such trying times, politicians should prioritize people over personal or partisan agendas.

Racism is found in all political parties – even in those that rail the most vocally against it. Often, thunderous complaint is focused on gaining attention as opposed to sparking real change. As Americans, we have the right to vote for whoever we believe best represents us. Political parties also have the right to ask for our votes when they represent our interests. Voting should also be free of racial bias, but unfortunately, it is not. I have been asked countless times as to why I do not vote Democrat. My response has always been that I do not make political decisions based on racial identity. I vote for the platform that I feel represents my values.

I was invited years ago to a Republican Party dinner where President George Bush Senior would be speaking. A white friend who was a lawyer invited me in order to introduce me to the Republican Party because he assumed that I was a Democrat. I agreed to go in order to listen to the President and see if the Republican Party shared my values. Before the dinner began, a female Republican senator approached me and asked where the bathrooms were. I looked puzzled, and the lady said "Aren't you a waiter here?" I politely responded that I was not a waiter, that I had been invited to attend and that I was hoping to ascertain if the Republican Party welcomed black people. The lady turned and walked away, perhaps looking for someone else to show her where the bathrooms were. The senator's comment was racist and off-putting to someone who was looking to join the Party. However, my lawyer friend overheard everything and apologized for the lady. In spite of my initial encounter, I found that the President and I did indeed share many values. The senator was not going to color my view of white people and Republicans. The friend who invited me knew me well as a person, and not as a "black" person. Our friendship was based on shared commonalities – we weren't "token" friends of other races. I realized back then that we must fight racism with knowledge and grace as opposed to reacting with hate and revenge.

Another issue that we are facing right now is the battle over symbols that have racist associations, such as statues of controversial historical figures and the Confederate flag. I understand how these objects can be reminders of the pain of slavery. I am a trauma specialist and I understand how trauma affects the brain and can paralyze one throughout life. I have treated a lot of people with trauma for over 30 years and I have researched trauma and healing. Trauma can be (and needs to be) healed, as it can incapacitate a person to the point where no progress can be made. When such a point is reached, a person will respond to current life events as if a past trauma is ongoing. People who have Post Traumatic Stress Disorder will continue to be triggered by things that remind them of their trauma until they are able to work through that trauma. People around the world have experienced a great deal of trauma due to Western Colonialism, the first and second World Wars, Hitler's Holocaust against the Jews and other groups, and ongoing regional conflicts.

Nelson Mandela spent 29 long years in prison simply for asking for equal treatment. After his release and ascendance to the presidency, the first thing he did was to have dinner with the very white president who had presided over the Apartheid system that imprisoned him. Then he formed the *Truth and Reconciliation* commission for white and black people to meet in court rooms for mutual confession and forgiveness of the racial crimes that had been committed during the years of injustice. Mr. Mandela was a very wise man, and his suffering taught him that the best way to deal with the past is to leave it behind through a process of healing.

As a nation, we must find healthier ways to heal from the traumas of slavery and racial discrimination. While it is impossible to eliminate all triggers, we must let go of the pain that is devouring us. I often tell my clients who have experienced trauma that if they hold onto the past, they will pay the price of bitterness and anger themselves, while their abusers sleep soundly. The trauma victim does him or herself a great favor by healing the trauma and moving on.

If we had focused only on the racial injustices of our past, we wouldn't be where we are today. If I viewed all white people as oppressors, I would be unable to relate to white people in a healthy way. Being able to relate to all people is necessary for my own growth and prosperity. Letting go of the past is a must if we are going to move forward as a nation. It is not enough simply to talk about all of the issues without discussing strategies to deal with them.

If the media attend the discussions, it is important that they stick to reporting and not try to hijack the outcome of the meetings. While I believe in freedom of speech and oppose the censorship of journalists, I also see that there is problem when the media is blatantly partisan. The media has a duty to report evenly and provide each party with equal time and coverage even for those they may disagree with. I have heard some of journalists refuse to report on a certain politician because they disagree with them. That is not journalism but campaigning for a particular party. It is very disturbing to see how the media has fanned the flames of the protests by focusing on the most inflammatory scenes overlaid with opinionated narration. Certainly all Americans have the right to voice their opinions, but journalists have an obligation to report without bias. I fear that a meeting such as the one that I am advocating would be covered by the media in a biased fashion.

Above all, at a meeting between contending groups, politicians must be open to listening and learning in order to be able to formulate policies and laws that actually work. Lawmakers would likely ennact better laws if they have the opportunity to listen to feedback from the people who elected them. Some elected officials may be far out of touch from the daily lives of ordinary Americans. Some may have lived lives of privilege, and it would benefit them to gain understanding of the problems that people face every day.

Politicians are also currently very divided on so many issues, and I fear that the issue of racism will be politicized at the expense of the people. Certainly, as a democracy, contentious issues must be discussed before laws can be enacted to remedy them. I have lived in the USA for over 40 years now, and the polarization that I have observed in the last decade is greater than anything that I have seen before. The healing of the nation may need to start with our politicians. How can a divided leadership direct the mending of division when they themselves are in need of healing? Our politicians must mend their own rifts before they can be effective.

Chapter 7: The Many Faces of Racism

Racism reveals its ugly face in many areas of life such as education, the work place, sports and other areas. In education, racism can be devastating to minority students who would like to attend college, but due to unfavorable circumstances in their communities, are unable to. Some people, especially young people, may not understand the reasoning behind the adoption of "affirmative action" policies. Some colleges have complained about being pressured to provide disadvantaged minority students with equal opportunities and scholarships that take into account the hindrances that arise from their status in life. Affirmative action came into being due to the hurdles that members of minority groups must surmount in order to enter and/or pay for college due to racial inequality and the history of segregation.

When black students were "bussed" into white schools, the objective was to offer minority students opportunities to learn in a different environment. I believe that some of the unintended benefits of this was that students were able to form friendships with those of other races. These students were learning to become color-blind in spite of the possible racial prejudices of their parents. I am sure some of the teachers discovered that minority students could be just as smart as white students. Many likely recognized that there may have been certain circumstances that were interfering with the minority students' education that had nothing to do with their supposedly inherent inabilities to learn. In the past, problems with academic performance in the black community were often attributed to racial difference, when in fact poor learning environments and home structures were the primary factors.

In the past, minority students were often told that they had lower IQs, which led many of them to feel that they were not as smart as white kids. We often heard that black kids were not doing well in their exams or tests. However, no rational explanation was ever provided for such a supposed disparity. We now know that certain students learn differently and that the results of many tests are indicative of performance anxiety and cannot be considered objective measures of intelligence. Poor performance on a test does not correlate with unintelligence. Attempting to correlate minorities with the results of intelligence tests is a form of racism. However, endeavoring to understand the circumstances that affect the learning process will make teachers more effective.

Education has always been the backbone of civilization, and all citizens of a country must have equal access to education if they are going to contribute to the advancement of their society. Societies that have cohesive and integrated systems of education tend to do better than those with divided and segregated systems of education. On the other hand, I understand the reason behind the existence of all-black colleges. Due to the surrounding environment of racism and segregation, black people had to find ways to afford education that would enable them to succeed in an environment that was not antagonistic. However, continuing to segregate our educational systems may no longer be helpful as it can serve to polarize and reinforce stereotypes. If we want to create a society that embraces all races, we must focus on a college environment that welcomes and integrates students of all races. White and brown students should be welcome in formerly all-black colleges. We must not succumb to *reverse* discrimination.

Sports is also another important feature of American culture that has been affected by racism. As Americans we love sports — football, basketball, track and field, baseball, and many others. When I was a college student, I was trying to understand American football, as this sport was not played in my home country. I couldn't understand why these huge guys always piled up on top of each other. One day I was working at an auction and there was a football game on television. I asked my supervisor, a nice white guy, what was going on. He explained to me that the players were trying to stop the opposing team from moving the ball towards the end zone. He told me that in that particular play, the quarterback had handed the ball to the running back instead of throwing it. He then gave me a lesson on how important quarterbacks were to the game and how they had to have more intelligence than those who played the other positions. During another televised football game, I asked my supervisor why there were more black players than white. His answer was that black people were better athletes than whites, but that they weren't smart enough to play quarterback positions. After that, I started watching to see how many quarterbacks in professional football were black. The first one I saw was Doug Williams, who played for the Redskins. I know now that there were a few others before him. As I read about sports and race, I frequently encountered the notion that white people thought that black football players didn't have the intelligence required for the quarterback position. However, in the National Football League there are now many black quarterbacks, who have proven themselves just as effective as their white counterparts.

I recall the photo of Jesse Owen winning gold at the Olympics held in Munich, Germany. This caused a great to deal of consternation to Adolf Hitler, whose racist ideology held that no black man could defeat the superior white man. It is saddening that today there are still people who hold such views in regards to sports and other areas of life. Racism affects how people feel towards each other and is sometimes demonstrated when people compare athletes of different races. I was in South Africa when Tiger Woods was playing in a golf tournament. White South Africans believed that Ernie Els, a fellow white "brother," would beat Tiger. As I watched on TV from the airport in Johannesburg, I felt upset that the game was being racialized in spite of the fact that the two players saw it merely as a test of skill. I rooted for Tiger because he was an American and I was behind my fellow countryman. I also felt pride at the fact that Tiger, as a person of color, was disproving the racist notion that golf was a "white man's game."

Racism in sports is unreasonable but has deprived very talented black athletes of the same opportunities afforded to white players.

Fortunately, the world of sports has made giant strides in bridging the racial gap. Athletes themselves relate well with other players regardless of race. Part of this success is a result of them playing, traveling and competing together. This just goes to prove that learning about other people and spending time with them helps in to weaken the clutch that racism holds on society.

Racism has also greatly impacted the workplace. Minority workers want only to be treated the same way as white ones, with equal pay and opportunities for promotion. No one should be passed over simply because of their race. Of course, few managers would blatantly say that race is the reason why someone is passed over for promotion or a job opportunity. Some excuse other than racism is always proffered as justification.

Many years ago, a friend informed me that someone had submitted my name to be considered for a counseling position at a church that I had previously attended. My friend was told that I did not meet the criteria for consideration because white people would be reluctant to seek counseling from someone like myself. I told my friend that it wasn't true that white people would avoid seeking me out for counseling, because the majority of my clients at that time were white. It was very sad that someone who was qualified was denied a job simply on account of race.

Jobs are a very important part of any society. Everyone is aware that a strong economy is important to the well-being of a nation. The governmental responses to the ongoing pandemic have clearly demonstrated what happens when the economy is shut down. Jobs provide much more than a paycheck. They give us a sense of purpose, pride, accomplishment and value to society. When a person is not able work in a position that they desire, they are in danger of losing all the things I just mentioned above. Society must ensure that jobs are available to all who want them. Race should not be a deciding factor in who gets a job and who doesn't. In free societies, skills and qualifications should determine who gets which job. Some companies are conscious of racial issues and go out of their way to ensure that minorities have equal opportunities for employment and promotion. As a country, we have come a long way but could still do more to progress.

One of the ways to make progress is to emphasize job and career-oriented education in minority communities. There are many jobs and professions that have been traditionally seen as white-only, such as the position of football quarterback. On the other hand, some less-desirable jobs and professions are relegated to certain minorities due to racism. I don't believe that certain people should be limited to only specific jobs. Also, when it comes to choosing a professional path, children can be greatly influenced by the examples of their parents.

I was very encouraged to hear a young black girl tell me that she wasn't going to become a hair stylist or work in a fast food joint like the rest of her peers. I asked her why she felt that way, to which she replied that these seemed to be only jobs available for black people. I then told her that people will always be needed to work in salons and fast food joints, but that job choice should not be racially assigned. I often talk to young minority students about selecting professions and jobs. I challenge them to not accept the limits that racial prejudice or stereotypes might try to place on them.

Chapter 8: Defeating Racism

I like to think of racism as something to be defeated because I believe that it can be overcome. It *must* be defeated in the manner that epidemics are conquered. Right now the world is facing a real threat from COVID-19, and scientists are working around the clock to search for ways to defeat this horrible virus. I hope these protests have demonstrated the danger of allowing racism to fester. If the protests continue, we can only expect more devastation to ensue.

Last night as I was working on this book, I saw on the news that a young man was shot and killed by police at a Wendy's restaurant in Atlanta. I don't know all the facts, but from the video it appears that lethal force was not justified. The police had already confirmed that the man was unarmed during a pat-down. The young man reacted in terror and was only trying to get away. What thoughts, feelings and assumptions were going through his mind? I believe that both the police officer who fired the shots and the young man went into the "fight or flight" mode, and as a result, a precious life was lost. That man was someone's son, friend or brother and deserved to live like everyone else.

It is unnecessary to provide further examples of racism, as by now, practically everyone has seen enough incidents from the protests to be well-aware of the problem. I also think that for protesters to persist is like beating a dead horse. It would be more effective for them to draw down the protests and allow leaders to start talking about solutions. To continue destroying property and burning buildings would weaken the message that they have already communicated. Burning down Wendy's restaurant doesn't send a message that we want equal justice. Just because a worker at Wendy's called the police doesn't mean that they intended for the police to kill the young man.

I wrote this book primarily to put forward some ways to improve the situation as opposed to fanning the flames of protests. I have heard the protesters say that they want to end racism, and I couldn't agree more with them on this point. But let's start focusing on that – once we see that our leaders are making an effort, let us give them a chance to talk about the issues. If we continue to protest and engage in violence, we will inhibit opportunities for discussion.

How do we end racism? Are the police and/or government responsible for finding the solution? If I am correct in stating that racism is ingrained in people's belief systems, then it's fair to say that the responsibility lies with us, the People. We are the ones that must have a change of heart. Everyone, from the President of The United States to the average person on the street, holds onto their own beliefs about race. Rather than pointing fingers, let each of us search our own hearts. If an individual truly desires to be color-blind, he can be. Those that do not know how to proceed can learn. There are many educators in our society who are prepared to jump into action and help people learn to relate to individuals of other races. I am sure that numerous books and resources are also in the works at this moment. These protests have been a huge wake-up call.

Many look to the government to remedy the issue of racial division. I agree that the government certainly can make laws that thwart racist behavior. Laws must also be enacted to protect people from racially-motivated police brutality and mistreatment. The government can also enforce anti- discrimination laws in our schools, workplace and sports. However, the government cannot control the human heart or legislate one's morality. If racism comes from the heart, it is the heart that must be transformed, which I believe is possible. We have observed how easy it was for diverse groups to mobilize and unify in protest. Surely, we can also mobilize to promote racial understanding and harmony. Action that arises from the heart is more powerful than that which is external. The world has seen the power of love demonstrated before, and if we embrace love, it will unify us. By love and unification, I do not mean the "power of positive thinking" or "feel-good" notions that are prevalent today. I am not even talking about religion, but rather the human will to truly desire a better world and society.

Classes and meetings can be organized that focus on learning about and meeting with those of other races. If we can devote so much time and money into going to the gym and other pastimes, we should certainly be able to invest in methods to combat racism. Yet another avenue would be for our government to form a council or department focused on race relations. If our government prioritizes national unity, sure investment in such a department would be in their interest. Classes or meetings should include people of all races to represent the true melting pot that is America. It is my opinion that racist beliefs are what drive some people to transform America into a segregated or even racially homogenous society.

While I am not suggesting that America dismantle our immigration policies, everyone who *legally* comes to America should be embraced. Those coming to join us in this great country should be committed to its values, which include embracing everyone. In fact, most Americans originated from somewhere else. The ancestors of white Americans all emigrated here from Europe. For the most part, they do not refer to themselves as "German-Americans" or "Swiss Americans" but simply as Americans. While I support honoring and preserving one's cultural heritages, all American citizens are first and foremost *American*. We can truly end racism in this country if we firmly believe in One America for all its citizens. Our founding fathers supported immigration since they were immigrants themselves.

Schools should incorporate classes on race throughout the course of college and graduate school, beginning with the first year. While some may think that this is an extreme suggestion, we must consider some important facts. Our society is becoming more interracial by the day, and we could have even more problems 30 to 40 years from now when whites become a minority. Therefore, the issue of racial prejudice must be dealt with now. The message of freedom has brought many diverse peoples here and will continue to do so, and we must be prepared for the demographic shift.

Before we continue the discussion about racial injustice and police brutality, we must all recognize that we have a personal responsibility to extirpate racism from within ourselves. Many people do not realize that they have racist beliefs until someone else points it out to them. If we focus only on what *other* people need to do to end racism, we will never succeed.

Racism is a problem of the heart, but when racism boils to the surface as criminal action, the law must step in as well. We already prosecute hate crimes, which helps to deter further obvious racist actions. However, how could hate crimes be prosecuted if the police were defunded and there is no one to arrest criminals? Hate crimes are the worst manifestation of racism. The people who commit hate crimes are most likely not going to change behavior without some serious consequences such as fines or imprisonment. These people are often the most resistant to influence by community education. Most of them are what we call psychopath – those who lack the conscience and remorse that prevents the majority of people from harming others. Our conscience tells us to be kind to one another, to help each other without regard to race.

Those who attend church or are familiar with the Bible have probably heard the story of the Good Samaritan (Luke 10:25-37). It is a parable that Jesus told to illustrate what it means to be a good neighbor. In the story, a certain man was attacked by thieves, was robbed of all his possessions, and was beaten and left for dead. A priest passed by and saw what had happened to the man but did not offer help. A Levite then came by, but kept his distance. Then the Samaritan came by, a man from a race that the Judeans considered to be unclean. He helped the wounded man and even took him to an inn and paid for his lodging. Jesus told the story because he had been asked by one of the teachers about being a good neighbor. If we are to end racism, we must have the perspective of the Good Samaritan and offer help to those of other races when they are in need.

Ending racism will not happen overnight – it is going to be a process that requires a great deal of time and work. If we try to remedy racism with rushed and poorly-conceived solutions, the problem will resurface. I know as Americans, we are not the most patient people in the world. We seem to prefer quick and easy solutions even to very complex problems. Sometimes we think that there is always a ten-step process to solving everything. It is probable that the solution will be found only after scores of difficult steps that we must take as individuals and as a nation. Again, I contend that our political leaders must lead the way by showing us that they, too, are serious about bringing us together. They start this process by demonstrating that they can overcome their political and racial biases towards one another.

Chapter 9: Police Reform

I am neither a lawyer nor a politician. I have never studied criminal justice or law enforcement science. My knowledge of this topic consists only of what I have observed in my role as an expert witness in certain legal cases. Many of the cases for which I testified did not involve the police, but I have seen cases that were totally based on the evidence that police investigations found or collected. Some of these cases resulted in wrongful convictions. Although the responsibility for a conviction lies in the hands of the prosecutor, the preliminary steps begin with police work. I have heard from many protestors that the police, rather than the accused, are often the biggest problem. I continue to hear protesters express the sentiment that police actions are definitely an issue. On the other hand, I haven't seen much focus on injustice in the criminal system, which I think that for some people, is implicit in the issue of racial injustice.

Our justice system needs to be reconsidered, as black people seem to be disproportionately targeted and convicted. Many black people have been found guilty but exonerated years later through DNA evidence. This indicates that the justice system itself at times functions with a bias against black people, which in my opinion arises through racism. Certainly, something has to change. The same bias that is displayed in courtrooms is demonstrated when police arrest black people based on the assumption that they are either violent or prone to criminal behavior. We also often hear of instances when a white person falsely identifies a black person as a perpetuator in a line up.

While reforming the justice system has been discussed before, inequalities persist to this day. It is unlikely that police reform alone will rectify the inequity in the justice system, as policing bias is only one side of the problem. The trial, conviction and sentencing processes subsequent to an arrest must also be factored into the equation. All aspects of the justice system must be scrutinized if we want to address racism in its totality. By reform, I simply mean changes that may help improve relations between communities and police. Racism has created dangerous conditions for both certain ethnic communities and officers, especially for officers who are not racist. A few bad apples can endanger all.

We must find ways to mitigate the danger brought about by unnecessary escalation and use of force by police. Police education is a good place to start. What is covered in the curriculums of police academies? The curriculum should incorporate courses that focus on communication skills. Some officers lack the skill to calmly address a civilian. People dislike being talked down to or being accused. Innocent citizens also dislike being approached by an armed police officer who displays an attitude of aggression and suspicion. The many people with mental illness who can be found in the streets are also very vulnerable, as they are not in their right mind. These people can often appear as if they are going to engage in aggression or questionable activities. Our police officers must also be educated on mental illness, and learn to identify and avoid escalation with those who could already be in a hyper-aroused, agitated or delirious state.

As a mental health professional, I have called 911 on occasion when a person with mental illness loses control or indicates a desire to harm themselves, family members, or others. In these cases, the police will respond either alone or alongside the fire department. One of the very first times I had to make such a call, I was shocked that they handcuffed the poor frightened woman. I protested the action and requested that the officers un-cuff her, as she had not committed any crime and only needed to be transported to the psych hospital. The officers over ruled me and said it was policy to handcuff people in these scenarios. The problem with such policies is that they are put in place with no understanding of mental illness and often exasperate problems when applied to those with mental illness. In this case that I related above, the actions of the police resulted in the loss my client's trust, which I later had to rebuild.

Another incident that occurred in my office involved a female client who was carrying a knife. She asked me if the knife was sharp enough to kill her children without causing too much pain. This was a very serious situation that put the lives of several innocent children in mortal danger. In my profession, I was restricted to disclosing this information only to the police. I called the police station that was located near the family of the client and requested intervention. An officer told me that there was nothing they could do since she had not threatened anyone directly. This response indicated to me that that officer had no training in handling such cases.

It would also be helpful for police academies to provide courses in race-relations. Officers must be familiarized with the racially diverse communities that they serve. At the beginning of this book, I gave the example of how the Minneapolis police chief communicated well with protesters. He was able to resonate with the people because he knew the community and how to talk with them. He acquired these abilities by living in the black community. When we send white officers into an ethnic community that they are unfamiliar with, we can expect problems to arise. Earlier, I suggested recruiting officers from their own communities and pairing them with another officer from a different ethnic group so that they can learn from each other.

We should also ask the question as to whether the duration of police training is adequate for mastery of the topics. Most professions require a four year degree, and some require an additional graduate degree. Other professions require one to pass extensive exams and/or obtain licenses. Most licensing also requires periodic renewal by completing requirements of continuing education. If police work is important, shouldn't the education and the training reflect that? We thoroughly train our teachers, so should we not do the same for police officers? If we don't require much training or education for police officers, we shouldn't be surprised when some of them don't perform to our expectations. I question the wisdom of police academies that consist of only several months of training. Policing consists of more than brute force, physical fitness and mental toughness. These attributes often make it seem like these are the essence of policing. While these qualities are necessary, many situations do not necessitate brute force, while others are exacerbated by it.

When my now 23 year old was a small child, I was walking with her to our car after a festival in our city, and we encountered a police officer controlling traffic and the crowds of people who were crossing the street. I held my child's hand and attempted to cross with other people as the officer motioned for us to cross. Then he decided to stop half of the group, but I didn't see his hand stopping us, and I kept walking. That officer yelled at me in anger and frustration, which made me upset, as the yelling was also directed at my child. I stopped and walked back to the side of the street that we had come from. I then waited until most people had crossed and the officer wasn't busy. I then walked up to him with my child in hand and asked if I could talk to him. Clearly I wasn't confrontational. I told him that it was not necessary to yell at me like he did and that it uncalled for. He quickly became angry and put his hand on his gun. That was not a very professional way to respond to a peaceful citizen.

We must also investigate the screening process of police applicants. Other professional entrance processes incorporate rigorous entrance exams and score requirements for acceptance. How rigorous are the requirements for those that wish to enter a police academy? To me, such a critical profession that can potentially endanger both the lives of the public and officers should implement every precaution. The screening policies for police academies should be as rigorous and thorough as possible. Certain people should be ineligible for policing positions for the sake of community and officer safety. Screening can help to ensure that only appropriate candidates are admitted. During the process, some applicants can also receive help with certain issues that may make them vulnerable to the stressful situations that come with police work.

I am concerned that some people with Post Traumatic Stress Disorder (PTSD) enter the police force without proper treatment for the condition. Along with my friend, Herschel Walker, a former NFL running back, I once visited a police academy in Texas. We learned that a number of students were soldiers returning from combat. I was happy to hear that we were employing our veterans. But I was also concerned about their potential for having problems with reactions triggered by PTSD when faced with potential violence on duty. I wondered what services were provided to them by the police force for PTSD-related issues. What would happen to them if they lost control and PTSD affected their work? Would they lose their jobs? Would the stigma of having problems hinder them from seeking out assistance?

Police officers have a difficult and often stressful job. I don't know how much they get paid, but they deserve to be treated well by their employers. They risk their lives every time they leave their houses to go to work. The issue of racism has made it even more dangerous to be a police officer. I do not often hear expressions of appreciation for police officers – right now, they are predominately criticized. We live in a society that is dominated by the media. Unfortunately, our media at this time tends to empathize with the mob as opposed to looking at things objectively. I think the media has unintentionally crucified all police, even though all police are not corrupt.

Police are human, and at times they need help, encouragement, and positive motivation. When Herschel travels around the country speaking at military bases, he encourages service members to seek help when they need it. I would suggest that others with good hearts and relevant experience that can be utilized in police training follow his example.

As I have stated before, I am not a politician and won't make any legislative suggestions, but I will suggest that our legislators take into account the sentiment of the people before rushing to enact cosmetic changes that fall short of real remedies. It appears to me our government is divided; one side touts the progress they have made in combatting racism while the other screams that nothing has been done. I think that we should seek to find middle ground and balance. We can acknowledge that while some positive changes have taken place, more still needs to be done. Talk is cheap, and people want to *see* real change.

We cannot discuss police reform apart from also discussing behavioral reform of the general public's perception of police. I have seen signs in people's yards that say "We back the blue", which simply means those people support the police. These people realize the need for the police and want police to know that they are supported. We can safely assume that such people are supporters of fighting crime. Police probably feel safer driving around in communities where they know that they are supported.

On the other hand, there are other communities where the police don't feel safe. Those of us who are minorities can also feel unsafe around the police. Even though we may have done nothing wrong, we can sometimes be harassed for no reason other than that we are different. A few years ago, I was walking back to my office from a Walmart when a police officer stopped me in his patrol car. He asked me if I had just left the police station which was only a few hundred yards from where I was walking. I answered that I had not been to the police station. He let me go, but stopped again and asked me if I was the guy who had just escaped from their custody carrying a grocery bag like the one I was carrying. I responded again that I had neither been to the police station nor escaped from their custody. When I finally arrived at my office, I reflected on what had occurred and realized that the officer didn't know anything about me but was just basing his actions on false assumptions. Trying to persuade him to reconsider his assumptions would have likely heightened his suspicion, and he probably would have arrested me. Simply refusing to argue with him and complying with his queries deescalated the situation.

I realize that it can be difficult to hold back from defending oneself when one is falsely accused and targeted. However, if we hope to end the conflict between police and the black community, we must teach our young people to comply and seek de-escalation. It would be difficult for a reasonable and professional police officer to escalate a situation where the suspect is calm and compliant. I also know there is a great deal of trauma in our black communities and that we can easily be triggered by aggression. The human brain can quickly spur one to run or defend oneself at even the slightest perception of danger, even when that perception is inaccurate. Police confrontation often only heightens such perceptions.

We often hear of cases when people are shot in the back by police, which indicates that they were running away. People tend to run because they want to avoid capture or injury. In the world of trauma treatment, we often deal with what we refer to as *perceived* trauma that is based on expectation as opposed to reality. Essentially, the part of our brain that warns us of danger tells us that a particular situation could lead to trauma, even when the perception is incorrect.

When I came to the US for my first semester in college in the US, a guerilla war was underway in Zimbabwe. There was a curfew in place from 6:00 PM to 8:00 AM in certain rural areas that were designated as "protection keeps." Thousands of people were packed into these small areas so that the military would be able to pursue guerilla fighters during the hours of curfew. If you were black and found roaming outside the "keeps" during those hours, you could be shot and killed because the military assumed you were a guerilla fighter.

When I was still in Zimbabwe, I was on my way to visit my mother who was living in one of the "keeps." My car broke down. It was getting dark and I knew that I was not going to make the curfew. So I did the only thing that I knew to do and found a place to hide on a hill. I didn't sleep well at all because I could hear a helicopter flying around the hill. I was very glad when 8:30 AM arrived and I heard people talking and going about their business. I could also hear army trucks rumbling down the roads. I walked back to my car, got it running, and continued on the drive to see my mother. I prayed all the way that I wouldn't hit a landmine, as there were many land mines on the roads that maimed and killed many people.

Three or four years later, I was playing flag football at college in the US and heard a helicopter flying above us. Without thinking, I quickly ran to the dormitory without explanation. Once I got inside, I realized that there was no need to run. I wasn't in the Zimbabwe bush anymore and the helicopter did not pose a threat, as no one else was running. I ran back to the game and told my team that I had just gone for a drink of water. After the game, I told my roommate the truth. He said that the helicopter was a just news chopper for the KVIL station, and we both had a good laugh.

There is so much trauma in our communities that the mere sight of police can make us feel unsafe. Even when police are not behaving in a threatening way, past traumas induce perceptions of threat. Therefore, we must take action in our community to heal from policing trauma so that we can respond appropriately around police that do not engage in oppression. We cannot expect the police to change their behavior if we do not change ours.

In our black communities, we should educate and encourage our young people to feel safe around the police. One prominent sports figure has told his sons that they need to comply with police directives when stopped by them. The sports figure is looking out for the well-being of his children, but his message is applicable to all people and particular to all young men. We need to encourage them to remain calm and cooperative when stopped or questioned by the police. If they comply and cooperate, the police will have no excuse to act unprofessionally. If we remain calm, it will be much easier to defend oneself in the courtroom in cases where police cross the line. Arguments should be reserved for the courtroom as opposed to the street where there is no judge to listen.

Our elders must also step up and lead us in the fight for equal justice. They have been around longer than young people and have often experienced worse racial injustices. We need our elders to demonstrate to our young people how to be responsible citizens in their own communities. We should respect and listen to our elders. We must earn the respect of our parents and grandparents so that they can be proud of us. When elders show up at a meeting or event, all young people should stop and listen to what they say.
As a young boy, whether we were playing, arguing or engaging in mischief, if just one elder passed by, we would immediately stop what we were doing. Our respect for our elders was profound. I strongly believe that here in America we strongly value our *African-American* identity, which I, as African-American as one can be, consider to be a respectable quality. If we are truly African-American we should love and respect our elders and communities.

An American politician once quoted an African proverb: "It takes a village to raise a child." I couldn't believe hearing that, because here in America we don't know what that really means. If our black communities were to practice that proverb, we would transform our community and America as a whole. The message of the proverb is that one should love and protect every child as they do their own. I believe that every black person here has it within themselves to take the proverb to heart. I have seen and sensed it in many other black people. There is a certain feeling I experience that says you are my brother or you my sister. If we were to tap into that, we would influence the whole country to move towards kindness and caring for one another. We would also reduce much of the pain and anguish that we often dish out to one another in our own community. I would strongly suggest that if we begin with reforming our own communities, we would compel the government to initiate lasting reform, as opposed to some of the superficial proposals that I have heard from our political leaders.

Chapter 10: Moving Towards Racial Equality

One of the primary beliefs of the racist is that all people are not equal. Some racists actually believe that some people were *created* superior and others inferior. Many years ago when I was attending Bible school in Southern Africa, a fellow student and I went to visit one of our favorite adjunct teachers, Brian Atmore. Mr. Atmore was not an American missionary. He was a white Rhodesian and it was the white Rhodesians who were practicing racial discrimination in the country. Brian and his wife both spoke Afrikaans, a language spoken by people of Dutch descent. Brian was a very enthusiastic preacher and loved all people without regard to race. He invited my friend Pagiel and myself to have tea with him at his house. At the time, only American missionaries were known to do something of this nature. It was risky for him, because the church he pastored, an all-white church, wouldn't have approved.

During our tea time we discussed topics related to preaching that all the three of us loved. My friend Pagiel, who had a background in the Dutch Reformed Church asked Brian if the church's teaching concerning creation was correct. The church taught that there were two accounts of creation in Genesis. That teaching claimed that black people were created in the first event described in Genesis 1:1-2, but that God had to create humans a second time ("Now the earth was formless and empty, and darkness was over the surface of the deep..."). This belief went on to say that Adam and Eve were white and the second creation was good. Brian laughed at this belief and stated that although he was unfamiliar with it, that there were some liberal theologians with very bizarre beliefs. He assured us that all races arose from Adam and Eve and that all men are created equal.

Racial inequality lay at the heart of the evil perpetrated by the Apartheid system. Racial inequality is also at the heart of racism.

There cannot be no racial harmony without racial equality. Racial diversity can, in fact, co-exist alongside racial equality. People can even demonstrate some preference for their own racial group in such a case. Racial equality is not about being the *same* in every respect; rather, it is an equality of value and social standing.

Many years ago, I went to the American embassy while visiting a foreign country. They asked me for proof of citizenship. As I entered the building. I observed several white people inside and was glad to be among fellow Americans. Their race was irrelevant to me. I felt at home because these were my people based on our common citizenship. Our standing in the embassy was equal, even though we were of different races. It was amazing how everyone greeted each other and asked each other which part of the US they were from. When I returned home through the Dallas Fort Worth airport, I also observed the great diversity of citizens passing through Customs. The passport was an equalizer. To see this in action brings to mind an image of the society we could be living in if we are able to eliminate racism.

The big question remains: *how* do we achieve racial equality? Some would argue that racial equality has already been achieved in America. While I agree that on paper this is true, situations often arise that suggest we still have a ways to go. I now would like to suggest some ideas as to how we can proceed in the quest for true equality. Some of the ideas have to do with the responsibilities that we the people have. This doesn't mean that government has no responsibility – it has an enormous responsibility from the legislative side. However, government will change nothing if we the people don't ask for it. I understand that protesting is one way to pressure the government for change. However, as I have said before, protesting brings attention to a problem but does not solve it. Sometimes relentless and unending protests can backfire. We the people must seize the moment and coherently ask for very specific kinds of changes to be made – the process of which can only happen during meaningful dialogue. The People also have leaders who can sit down with government officials and discuss the issue of racial inequality.

We should not assume that government officials really understand racial inequality, as they often live lives of power and luxury far removed from their constituents. It really doesn't matter which party they belong to. The notion that the Democratic Party is the party for black people is naïve, and the true agenda of a party is to serve *the politicians* who are in power or seeking election. There is no party that black people should be compelled to support. Black people need to be able to speak for themselves rather than rely on one political party to speak for them. We had a black President for two terms, yet racial inequality remains. Even if Obama strongly desired change, he was limited by the structures of the government. To this day, we have only two primary political parties that are at war, each of which tries to prevent the other from taking any action. An African proverb says, "When elephants fight, the grass is harmed." This is so true for us, the People, as well. When the two political giants fight, we are the ones who are caught in the middle. It's about time that we speak out about this.

We should appoint representatives from our communities that we trust and who are also credible enough that the government is compelled to listen to them. One of the first responsibilities we have as a people is to organize a well-articulated proposal of what we are asking for. Such a proposal could include:

1. Identifying areas of life that we feel are impacted by racial inequality and preparing examples of this.
2. Demonstrating what racial equality would look like for us.
3. Recognizing areas where there have been improvements in racial equality. Many people are unwilling to listen to criticisms alone that do not also acknowledge advancements.

4. We must remain calm and avoid making demands that are superficial and/or irrelevant.

For more clarification on point 4, asking that certain offensive statues be removed won't change anything about racial inequality. Don't get me wrong – slavery and the civil war can be painful reminders to us. However, removing all those reminders will do little or nothing to bring about racial equality. On the other hand, why not ask for statues of historical figures that have special meaning to us? That, to me, would be a much more sensible approach. We must remember our history, the good and the bad. I can tell you. Reminders are less offensive than experiencing racial inequality in the here and now. It makes no difference to me if a statue remains standing as long as the oppression that the individual may have stood for is no longer an issue.

Working to heal wounds from the past is important and can positively affect the present and the future, but hanging onto pain from the past helps nothing. Someone who comes from an abusive marriage will carry those wounds into a new marriage. We certainly could not expect such a consecutive marriage to be successful, if the past is allowed to affect the present.

When I shared my ideas for this book with a friend, he asked me some tough questions. Why did I want to write this book? Could I offer any new insights when there are thousands of other black people even more qualified to speak on this topic of racism? I thought about my friend's questions before answering. After I had gathered my thoughts, I told him that I was simply playing my part in responding to something that I had known since childhood. I also wanted to convey some of the ways in which I personally overcame and healed from racism. I told my friend that it didn't matter that there may be thousands of other better qualified people. My story is unique and I wanted to share it. I also believe that even one individual can have the power to make a big difference. In my line of work, I don't focus on numbers or particular groups of people. My focus is on that one individual who is sitting in front of me for that hour. During that hour, he or she is the most important person, and I focus on what I can do to help improve that person's life. I believe the world is changed one person at a time. If only one person reads this book and has a change of heart concerning issues of racial equality or harmony, then I will be satisfied.

Because we are discussing significant societal change, government participation is crucial. Those in power are the ones who can actually write the laws to bring about change. We are literally asking the law makers to enact laws that enforce racial equality and do away with any old laws that inhibit or neglect it.

Many businesses post notices claiming that they are "equal opportunity employers." However, merely posting a sign or completing paperwork doesn't necessarily mean that a business actually extends equal opportunities. How could this be enforced? If one were to sue a business due to discriminatory employment practices, what evidence and precedents exist to support such a case? Even with all legal provisions in place, businesses *are* able to practice discrimination. There seems to be no truly heart-felt desire to treat minorities as equal. Racism runs deep and influences more than we are willing to admit. Legislation must *clearly* protect minorities from discrimination playing a role in opportunities and promotions. Again, though I am not a politician, I can certainly point out considerations that should be taken into account when anti-discrimination laws are put in place. The consequences of discrimination should be of such a nature as to motivate businesses to *want* to comply with the law.

Earlier, I discussed racism in sports and the tendency of the NFL to relegate black players to non-quarterback positions. To be effective in that situation, an anti-discrimination law should have significantly penalized offending teams. As opposed to merely being slapped with a fine, in such a case a team could be denied draft picks or suspended from a game. For a well-off business, a fine is a trivial matter, but non-monetary sanctions cannot be overcome without compliance. On the other hand, businesses could also be rewarded for following such a law.

Chapter 11: Moving towards Racial Harmony

I chose to discuss racial equality first, because when racial equality is achieved, racial *harmony* naturally follows. Harmony arises from the heart as opposed to forced legislation. A very big part of why there is little racial harmony in places today is due to the pervasiveness of racism, which engenders racial inequality. Racism deluded white people into believing that they were superior, from the era of slavery in Africa to the colonial days. Supremacism held that white people were better at everything since they brought new technology and knowledge to the African continent. The knowledge of the African people was deemed uncivilized. While schools, hospitals and knowledge that Europeans brought to Africa was much appreciated, these contributions are not a justification for an attitude of superiority. Diverse ethnic groups face problems that require different kinds of knowledge.

Racism sprouted in America as Native Americans were driven from their own lands onto reservations. Their way of life was also different from that of Europeans, but that does not mean that Native Americans were inferior. Their treatment by Europeans was wrong, and it's about time that we as a people begin recognizing that all peoples are equal. Differences in appearance do not justify concepts of racial superiority. People who feel that they are treated with indifference or hatred will not be able to truly get along with those who perpetuate racist behavior. On the other hand, those who feel threatened by violence will not be able to get along with people that they feel pose a threat.

Just yesterday, I was reading what the leader of the Black Lives Matter movement in New York (Mr. Hawk Newsome) had to say about threats of violence:

"If this country doesn't give us what we want, then we will burn

down this system and replace it."

It is rhetoric like this that hinders progress in achieving racial harmony. One who reads Mr. Newsome's statement might believe that his sentiment is shared by all members of the movement. While other leaders in the movement do *not* condone violence, it is hard to know how many *do* think and feel like Mr. Newsome. Such attitudes are troubling to those of us who love peace and order. We want to see change happen too, but as I have stated repeatedly, only meaningful dialogue will bring about change. Change cannot be brought about through "burning down the system." I wonder how Mr. Newsome plans to replace a system of government that has been in place for the entire history of this country. I understand the pain and anguish expressed by Mr. Newsome and others like him, but as a leader, he must allow his mind, rather than emotions, to guide him. While heightened emotions are not bad, they often can override good reasoning and judgment. The path to racial harmony must lie in sound reasoning and judgment to make the decisions that will affect change. As I have already said, we won't get there through protest alone. In fact, the longer the protests continue, the less chance we have for a peaceful and effective resolution.

How do we begin to work towards racial harmony within the framework of racial equality? Racial harmony is built on several pillars. The first pillar is that of knowing and accepting people of other races. How can that be done? We must leave our comfort zones and seek to know other people. As human beings, we often hold onto preconceptions about others simply because we do not know enough about them. Returning to the story of my previous father-in-law: when his daughter broke the news to him that she wanted to marry me, he became very upset and told her that I would be lazy and a failure in life. For three years, he wouldn't have anything to do with me. When he was challenged by his brothers who had taken the time to get to know me, he began to change his mind. After accepting me into his home and getting to know me, things started changing. I remember the first time he took me fishing, he learned that I knew a lot about life in both the city and wilderness. He learned that I grew up working as hard as he and his brothers did, and he started respecting my work ethic. When he realized that I respected him and all people, he told his friends what a good son-in-law he had. Even deep-seated racism can dissipate when people learn about others.

Learning about others must occur on a voluntary basis; it cannot be forced. As I stated before, one cannot legislate morality or matters of the heart. I believe that there are enough good people here who would like to see this country united. Such unity could begin with the people choosing to get along and set aside their racial divisions. We should also refuse to let our politicians divide us through their partisan politics. We can organize community events to facilitate interaction with those who are different from us. We can start even now during the COVID-19 by doing these online. Starting online may prove to be even more effective than real-world meetings, as those people who may be shy or fearful may be more open. Such events can follow the format of online "town hall" meetings such as those that have recently become widespread. Whenever the pandemic is over, we can transition to holding such events in person. We would be doing ourselves a great favor by turning our energy to positive activism. We have heavily invested in protest, but now we must learn to get along with each other. I can promise you that the power in positive steps towards unity is greater than that of creating havoc and division.

We have so many resources that we can utilize in this country. For example, the sports world is already taking steps towards harmony (to some extent), because they are brought together by sports. I would suggest that the sports world could lead the way since they are already engaged. They could hold meetings to facilitate the discussion of racial issues between athletes of different ethnicities. Again, those who participate must do so on a voluntary basis. Neither the NBA nor NFL should mandate participation. Some athletes are motivated to do amazing things to help their communities. I suggest that athlete activists make concerted efforts to help communities learn how to get along with people of other races. Some athletes hold training camps for kids, which can help by bringing together children of different races. I believe our children are far ahead of us when it comes to experiencing and understanding racial diversity. Camps based on voluntary participation can also be offered by schools. I am convinced that when children start reporting good experiences, others will want to attend as well.

Businesses and companies that are largely, racially homogenous can also offer temporary internships that provide opportunities for adults of different races to work together. This opportunity should be granted to all people, whether the company is dominated by whites, blacks or members of other races. Again, participation should be voluntary. Imagine what could happen if our politicians did something along these lines that facilitated the ability of members of opposing parties to share in work together. In the past, the two dominant political parties were not such mortal enemies as they appear to be now. Racial harmony will not be achieved overnight and will take time and work. America is a great country, but many people lost their lives making it what it is. Many committed to and sacrificed for great causes. As a country, we must return to the spirit that drove such people.

Chapter 12: The Role of the Church In Promoting Racial Harmony

The greatest story ever told about reconciliation is that of Jesus Christ. To the unreligious, don't worry – I will only summarize a story that is relevant to achieving racial harmony. Before his birth as a man, Jesus existed as God of creation. In the book of Genesis we learn that the world was created by God, who elsewhere in the Bible is described as God the father, God the Son (who is Jesus), and God the Holy Spirit. Jesus decided to come down to earth to make it possible for humanity to be reconciled to God. The Bible makes it clear that the gulf between humanity and God was so great that it was impossible for humans to bridge. Therefore, Jesus decided to make the journey and become human in all aspects. He lowered himself to the level of a slave and died so that today we can be called children of God.

The story of Jesus is the foundation of what we today call *the church*. The same Jesus Christ asks his followers to take on his mindset (i.e. *psychology*) when relating to other people. Therefore, the church ought to be the most equipped to promote racial harmony in the world. I am unhappy when I see racism in the church because it is one of the most un-*Christ*ian traits. I have already mentioned that I understand how cultural, linguistic, and geographical differences necessitate that certain people worship among those of their own ethnicity (which I see no problem with). However, a problem arises when people from another race are denied or discouraged from the opportunity to worship alongside others.

Racial issues have been present in Christian communities throughout history. In the early 1st century church, the Christian community was mostly Jewish and excluded non-Jewish people (who were referred to as "gentiles"). God challenged this thinking when He spoke to Peter (one of the leaders of the Christian movement). Peter was shown a vision of God asking him to kill and eat animals that were forbidden to Jews. In the vision, Peter responded that the animals were unclean and that he wasn't going eat something that *he* knew to be forbidden by God. God told him that He made those animals and to not call what God created unclean. The imagery of refusing certain foods was an analogy for Jewish discrimination against gentiles, who were also created by God. This vision changed the manner in which the early Christian leaders related to non-Jewish people. As the story continues, Peter and other Jewish believers cross their former racial and cultural boundaries (Acts 11:1-14). What can the Church learn from this story that can be applied in the 21st century?

From the stories of early Christian leaders, we can glean that the church leadership is not immune to racism. The leaders of the early church were perhaps the godliest men ever, and yet they were human and succumbed to the traditional racial perspectives that were prevalent at the time. Today, even the most religious people can easily be found holding onto racist beliefs and attitudes. Some leaders have had to acknowledge their own racist tendencies and ask God to help them. They have humbled themselves before God, who has helped them form new attitudes towards others. I also know that some churches are actively working to include people of other races in the congregation and even in leadership. Such churches are keeping pace with societal change and at the same time reflecting the Gospel of Jesus Christ, who bridged the gap between God and man. Such churches will do well in the rapidly approaching new reality of color-blindness and diversity.

In what other ways can the church contribute to ending racism? How can the church take a lead in modelling inclusion? Christians were the first people to experience true color-blindness when they embraced the love of God through Jesus Christ. The 1st century church that experienced Christ's love also experienced horrible persecution and terrible injustice at the hands of the Romans. Some were fed to wild animals alive while the Romans watched as a form of entertainment. Others were burned alive. They experienced a discrimination that was much more brutal, on average, than that today. However, in spite of all hardship, they did not lose faith or give up on fellowship.

Although what is happening in the world due to racism may not be seen as connected to faith, it is human suffering nonetheless. The Church can embrace people of different races with the love of God as a sign that they truly understand. Jesus himself said:

"A new commandment I give you: love one another. As I have loved you, so you must love one another. By this everyone will know that you are my disciples if you love one another." (John 13:34-35)

The bottom line is that the path to racial harmony must start in the church, which has both the mandate and resources. The primary resource of the Church is God himself through his Spirit who lives in every Christian. In what practical ways can the Church initiate racial healing? Leaders and pastors of influential churches can begin to cross their own racial divides. They can invite each other to their houses for fellowship and encourage their members to do the same. Church members can attend services at other churches with congregations of different races. Churches can also plan activities that facilitate interaction. Again, sports seems to be a natural unifier, and can be used as an ice-breaker prior to moving to the discussion of serious topics such as racism.

Churches can volunteer and join the movement for racial harmony without a need for coercion. It is my conviction that pastors who take the first step will be rewarded greatly as others follow their example. Many people don't really know where to begin to correct the issue of racism. Some pastors are generous enough to invite other pastors to preach at their churches. I know I am extremely proud that my pastor has invited preachers of many races to speak at our church. It would be difficult to label such a church or pastor as racist when action demonstrates time and again that all people are created equal. The church needs more pastors who value people for their abilities without regard to race. The Church can also cover racial issues in the classroom. Church members who are educated about racial issues may in turn educate others at work or wherever they go. As they interact with people of other races, they will set an example that is more powerful than words alone. This kind of approach to ending racism is among the most effective, as people respond to genuine love and acceptance.

As someone who grew up under some of the worst conditions of racial discrimination, I can tell you that unlike white Rhodesians, American missionaries convinced me that they were not racist. While they were not vocal about racial inequality and injustice, they demonstrated to us *how* people should treat others. In 1971, I was walking onto the campus of an evangelical Bible school as a freshman. A big white man walked up to greet me. He was somewhat intimidating due to his size, but he smiled and shook my hand, something that had never happened to me before. He was friendly, kind, and expressed interest as if I was someone special. Another black student was with me who had been showing me around, as he had already been at the school for a year. He saw that I was surprised and told me that these missionaries were truly committed to their students and that what I had experienced wasn't unique to this Reverend Sherwood.

During my second year at that Bible school I had to go to a remote mission station. I didn't know anyone, but I was assigned to work with an American missionary named Richard McCloy and his wife Mary Anne. I was nervous because I didn't know how they would treat me. However, my anxiety quickly disappeared, as this couple proved to be even friendlier than my professors at the bible school. On the first evening that I was there, they asked me to go over to their house and eat with them. I was shocked, because in my world we just didn't eat with white people. Sitting at the table, they made me feel like I was part of the family. Later, I would ride on a motorcycle with Rev. McCloy to visit people in a village, and I felt like we were preachers of equal standing. Dick Mc Cloy has always been a brother to me. To this day, that family and I are still in touch and sometimes we communicate in my native language, which they still speak fluently, even though they are now retired. These missionaries bridged the racial gap by living with people of a different race and learning our language and ways of life. Today, if you travel to parts of the world that have experienced missionaries of similar character, you will hear stories such as this.

While some missionaries have failed to bridge the gap due to racist beliefs, others who had no such beliefs have succeeded. It can be done in our present day. I suggest that both churches and the general community tap into these missionaries for ideas and methods as to how to reach out to people of other races. There is a tremendous mission field right here in America – that of bridging the divide between races. Missionaries, even those who are retired, may be eager for the opportunity to teach children how to grow and relate to others of all races.

There are many other avenues that churches can take to reach people of other races. I was very impressed that my church sent scores of people to area hospitals to encourage our first responders during the coronavirus pandemic. I remember watching one of the hospital administrators shedding tears because he was so appreciative of what my church had done for his hospital employees. Just think about what would happen if a group of people from a black church were to reach out to a white neighborhood. Or if a group of white people from a church were to reach out to a minority community. If such actions were taken all over the country, certainly it would attract some positive attention that would force our government to re-think race relations.

It appears to me that as protests become more ugly and violent, the Government doubles down on law and order, and it becomes a vicious cycle. In some parts of the world, popular uprisings have toppled governments. Here in America, we should think long and hard if we hope to burn down the system and replace it with the Black Lives Matter movement. The only realistic chance for meaningful change in the system is through dialogue.

I saw an article today in the news about certain black people leaving this country because they are fed up with the racism here. I wish I knew about these racism-free countries that they are going to! I suggest that instead of running that they consider exerting some effort to fix the problem here at home. If the objective of the protests is societal change, then running away will not contribute to the cause.

Epilogue

I often hear the phrase *"systemic* racism." I am unsure as to what all those who use the phrase believe it mean. I have heard some of our politicians state that there is no systemic racism in the country and then suggest that there is racism within a certain party. It is important that we understand what *systemic* means. An issue that is systemic permeates an entire structure. The concept of systemic racism implies that the structure of society itself is steeped in racism. If people who say that there is systemic racism in America mean that the very heart of our government is racist, then I would have to strongly disagree. If this was true, why have no representatives or senators done anything to address such a systemic problem? Certain politicians like to politicize issues for the purpose of winning an election when they actually don't believe a word of what they are saying. No, we don't have a racist government in this country. What we have is a society composed of individuals, some of whom are racist, and some of whom may be in positions of government. There are people in churches, businesses, sports, and even the justice system who hold racist beliefs and attitudes – but that doesn't make *everyone* a racist. As I mentioned earlier, racism is not just a problem of white people. Black people who are also capable of demonstrating racism towards white or brown people.

I understand that white racism is what sparked these protests. White police officers are often at the heart of the issue of police brutality, which killed George Floyd and others who died unjustly in police custody. I also understand that due to white racism, the justice system often wrongly convicts black people who may be innocent. I understand that white racism has colored how white society views black people in general. When you are a black person at the receiving end of racism, the whole governmental system can appear racist. However, the perception of systemic racism is not an accurate assessment of the situation, but rather an emotional reaction to the pain that we suffer due to experiences. When leaders in the black community abandon reason for emotional reactions, black people can appear unreasonable, which perpetuates the cycle of misunderstanding. In our black community, we have calm and reasonable people who should lead us in meaningful dialogue with our government in a serious attempt to end racism. I don't believe that we can fight racism by inflaming the situation, tearing down any statue that may remind us of slavery or reacting against everything that may have been associated with Southern heritage during the Civil War. I have said before, but I will say it again: we cannot continue to hold onto the pain of our past because we will become mired and never move on. Instead, we must focus on meaningful, practical change that can improve our experience of life.

I am encouraged to hear that police reform is being discussed around the country. In spite of the emotional cry to defund the police, the necessary police departments of many cities are still in place. We don't need to abolish the police; we need to *reform* them. I am sure that I am not the only person who made suggestions, but I have attempted to lay out some specific paths forward. The question is how to approach the powers-that-be in order to implement such changes.

We the people must organize and present our requests for dialogue to the government. We can lobby our representatives to speak with both houses to air our grievances and reasonable suggestions in a calm and collected manner. The controversial topic of police and justice reform should be taken seriously. I have stipulated one important change that should be implemented: effective screening of police applicants. Some of the negative traits that have been demonstrated by police officers should have been caught in screening. Some officers have a great deal of insecurity, and carrying a gun and a badge gives some a sense of power and significance that goes to their heads. Insecurities should be identified long before surfacing in the unnecessary harassment of innocent citizens. It is these types of insecurities that cause some of the officers to respond without self-control to the taunting that they sometimes face in the community. Those that taunt the police have their own insecurities that produce such immature behavior, but a trained officer should be able to brush it off and perform his duty.

In this country, the media has a great deal of power that can serve as a catalyst in this effort, but unfortunately, journalism has been linked with partisan politics. Journalists have embraced a tendency to bring attention to ideas that they support. As I write this book, I can imagine the media hijacking some of these ideas. As you may have noticed, I have refused to favor either party in an attempt to make the other party look bad. If our media is interested in bettering the situation, they ought to report facts without blatant bias. As I have pointed out, some have gone on emotional rants against certain politicians as if the media were functioning as an extension of a political party.

The media of certain countries is sponsored and controlled by government and practically a mouthpiece of the political party in power. This should never be the case in a free country like ours. We the people should protest corruption in the media, which has appointed itself as the judge and jury rather than fulfill the obligation to observe and report news in a balanced manner.

The primary point of this book was not to highlight the existence of racism – the protests have pretty much laid bare the impact of racism on our society. We should now focus on taking action to *change* things. Protests can only go so far before people tire and the tactic begins to backfire. My greatest concern is that we keep on protesting in the absence of meaningful dialogue with the people that matter the most. Expecting the government to yield to the threat of protest and enact change without serious dialogue is unreasonable. I will not be surprised if the protests effect very little change. If we want significant change, there is a lot of work that must be done by everyone, as opposed to entrusting responsibility solely to government. We should know by now that our government tends to be caught in gridlock in Washington, and if we leave it up to them to do all the work, we may be waiting for a very long time. We must all take the responsibility to make our country better upon ourselves. We can begin by doing our part and conducting ourselves rightly in the struggle to end racism.

Bibliography

Ellis, A. (2015, December 23). Rational Emotive Behavior Therapy. *Counseling Today*.

Van der Kolk, B. (1987). Traumatic Memories. *Journal of Traumatic Stress*.

Van der Kolk, B. (1996). *Traumatic Stress*. New York: Guilford Press.

About The Author

Jerry Mungadze was born and raised in the country formerly known as Rhodesia in southern Africa, which is now Zimbabwe. Rhodesia was named by Cecil John Rhodes after a British explorer who came to the country and claimed that he discovered it in spite of the fact that it was inhabited by a people with their own system of government and civilization who built an amazing structure out of stone with no cement: *Zimbabwe*, meaning the "big house of stone."

The country has one of the Wonders of the World: Victoria Falls, which was named after the Queen of England, even though the people of that country had a name for it which was most appropriate. The waterfalls look like smoke and it also thunders, and the local name for it was "The smoke that thunders." The colonial system led to one of the most severe implementations of racial discrimination at the time: *Apartheid*, which discriminated against black people. These were the conditions that Jerry Mungadze was born and raised in, and where he gained a deep understanding of racial discrimination.

He served as pastor and evangelist in Zimbabwe before coming to America for further education. He graduated from Dallas Bible College in 1982 with a Bachelor of Science in Bible. He then graduated in 1984 from Dallas Theological Seminary with a Masters in Bible. Then in 1990, he graduated from the University of North Texas with a PhD in counselor education.

Dr. Mungadze has been a practicing clinician for around thirty years in the field of psychological trauma. He has traveled to speak about trauma and related topics in many countries including Canada, Australia, Germany, The Netherlands, Greece, South Africa, Ghana, Kenya and all over the United States of America.

Made in the USA
Middletown, DE
13 February 2021